POLICY STUDIES IN EMPLOYMENT AND WELFARE NUMBER 14

General Editors: Sar A. Levitan and Garth L. Mangum

The Prison of Unemployment

Manpower Programs for Offenders

Robert Taggart III

The Johns Hopkins University Press   Baltimore and London

The Johns Hopkins University Press, Baltimore, Maryland 21218
The Johns Hopkins University Press Ltd., London

Library of Congress Catalog Card Number 72–3228
ISBN 0-8018-1424-3 (cloth)
ISBN 0-8018-1425-1 (paper)

Library of Congress Cataloging in Publication Data will be found on the last
printed page of this book.

231303

Contents

List of Tables

List of Charts

Preface

It is difficult to approach the subject of criminal offenders with objectivity. Everyone has their preconceptions about the criminal's debt to the community, about the possibility and value of salvaging these "prodigal sons," and about society's responsibility for the individual's failings. The issues of crime and the treatment of offenders have stirred heated public debate, and no citizen can remain impervious to the emotion and rhetoric which has been generated.

Yet objectivity is vital where the facts are disparate and difficult to interpret. There are no good comprehensive data about offenders. And most of what we have learned about their problems and the possible solutions to them is buried in a staggeringly diverse array of project findings. If any balanced judgments are to be made, bits of information must be pieced together from a variety of sources.

In such a piecing together, it is always a danger that preconceptions will influence perceptions. It is also a danger that the availability of information will be given precedence over its accuracy. Despite every effort at objectivity, it is likely that this paper on *manpower policies and programs for offenders* suffers from the bias of the author and the limitations of his knowledge.

Nevertheless, there are a number of individuals who helped provide more balanced judgment and more extensive vision. The staff of the Manpower Administration's Office of Research and Development, which initiated many of the experimental programs for offenders, offered information, insight, and editorial assistance, especially William Throckmorton, William Paschell, and Seymour Brandwein. Careful and critical readings were also provided by David Lewen, Eli Ginzberg, Charles Myers, and Sar Levitan.

This monograph was initially written as a background paper for consideration by the National Manpower Policy Task Force in preparing a policy statement on the same subject. Members of the Task Force offered comments and suggestions. Nevertheless, the ideas and interpretations are entirely those of the author.

The Prison of Unemployment

The Manpower Perspective

Society is acutely aware of the billions of dollars it loses each year to crime and of the billions it must spend for police, courts, and corrections institutions. But another equally significant cost is rarely recognized: the massive waste of human resources. There are now nearly six million arrests each year. State and federal prisons contain around two hundred thousand inmates, with about eighty thousand entering and leaving annually. Local jails and other institutions contain another two hundred thousand, with a rapid turnover so that many hundreds of thousands pass through them every year. Nearly a million more juveniles and adults are under supervision in the community on probation or parole. Offenders thus constitute a sizeable minority of the population. And all too frequently, especially in the case of those who are arrested, found guilty, and sent to jail, their economic and social potential is squandered by them and by society.

Whether it is a cause or an effect of their criminality, offenders are generally failures in the world of work. If involved in illicit activities, they are often outside the labor force or working at peripheral and unstable jobs. If arrested, they may be suspended in limbo for months awaiting trial, losing their jobs or simply losing interest in work; or they may be detained in jail, in which case work is impossible. If the offender is sentenced to prison, he is likely to do little productive work for the length of his term; prisons have their own industries and provide much of their own maintenance, but their "captive" labor force remains grossly underutilized. And once the offender is paroled or released, he is excluded from a number of jobs and given little help in finding his way back into the world of work. As a result, his earlier employment problems usually grow worse. From start to finish, the picture is one of wasted human resources—of skills and abilities which are underdeveloped and underutilized.

It is impossible to ignore the fact that offenders have violated society's laws. In some cases, criminality may be the product of their milieu or perhaps their belief that crime is the only way to survive in a repressive society. In other cases, it may result from serious mental or emotional difficulties. And some of the time, it is the result of unlucky circumstances and common human frailty. But the fact that criminal behavior is unacceptable and society must be protected from its effects, necessitates a system of punishment and detention. Though the police, court, the corrections systems may have many shortcomings, they at least crudely fill these vital purposes. Whatever changes are made, these must continue to be filled.

Nevertheless, concern with punishment and detention, or with improving the police, court, and corrections systems, should not detract from our concern over the wasted human resources. Society can only benefit from the full use of its manpower; and where it is feasible, efforts must be made to develop and utilize the economic potential of every citizen.

It is widely accepted that increasing employability is an important part of rehabilitating the offender. The conventional wisdom is that employment problems are a major cause of crime and that unless the offender can be prepared for and provided with a job he is likely to fall back into criminal behavior. From the "rehabilitationist perspective," employability must be improved to reduce recidivism. If, as a result, crime rates do not fall, then other strategies, such as counseling, behavioral motivation, and special institutional arrangements, may be needed.

The "manpower perspective" is slightly different. It views offenders as a highly disadvantaged clientele with serious deficiencies in the world of work. Like others with employment problems, they may need a wide range of services from education, training, and placement to counseling, health care, and financial support. For perhaps a majority of first offenders and even a substantial minority of those in prison or jail the only characteristics which distinguish them from other disadvantaged groups in the population is that they got caught. Though many will be rearrested because of inherent deficiencies, and some because of the lack of opportunities, the majority (at least of those who do not go to prison) will gradually adjust and abandon their criminal behavior. Their employment problems will not, however, be solved; and their potential as a human resource will not be realized. From this perspective, reducing recidivism should not be the major goal or criterion for success; if employability can be increased among offenders without reducing the proportion who recidivate and if this can be done at a reasonable cost, then the effort is worthwhile. Any decline in criminal behavior is an added gain since it will lengthen the period of increased employability.

The involvement of the offender with the police, court, and corrections system offers an opportunity for society to help him with his employment problems. Whether this is a good way of providing assistance or whether, in fact, assis-

3

tance should be provided, must be determined, among other things by the effectiveness of efforts to improve his employability. As in assisting other disadvantaged groups with manpower services, the questions become very practical. What services do offenders need? How can these be most effectively delivered within the existing institutional framework? What are the costs and benefits relative to other comparable efforts? How should programs for offenders be coordinated with manpower services for nonoffenders? Which individuals profit most from the known techniques? And what resources should be allocated to offenders which could alternatively help others in need?

The "rehabilitationist" and "manpower" perspectives are not mutually exclusive, but two ways of looking at the same nexus of social problems. However, most research has been carried out by those with the former rather than the latter orientation. It is only within the last few years that manpower analysts have begun to recognize offenders as a potential clientele and have begun to experiment with manpower services for this group. The results of their limited experience and experimentation are far from conclusive. Yet a lot has already been learned and must be translated into action. Specifically, decisions must be made on whether and how to expand manpower services for offenders from an experimental and demonstration level to an operational one. These decisions cannot be postponed until we know everything we would like to know. Society is now demanding that we do something about crime, and this means doing something for offenders. In recent years there has been a shift in public attitudes away from the strict concept of punishment toward the view that offenders are disadvantaged individuals who must be helped rather than hammered into shape. The role of manpower services in salvaging and utilizing this wasted human resource must be determined.

Offenders and the Corrections System

From the manpower perspective, the first analytical steps are to identify the "universe of need," to inventory its present and potential value as a human resource, and to examine the institutions which are responsible for its development and utilization. Much remains to be done on these preliminary tasks. Despite several comprehensive investigations and a few significant research efforts, little is known about the employment experience of offenders or the manpower aspects of corrections. As in so many cases, judgments must be made on the basis of disparate and all too limited evidence. But at least some general observations are possible, and the most salient characteristics of offenders and the corrections system can be identified. Three, in particular, deserve mention.

First, only a small proportion of offenders "progress" through all levels of the corrections system—from arrest, to trial, to jail, and to parole or outright release. At each level a number are provided alternative routes, with only a minority sent on to the next level. Essentially, the system functions as a sorting mechanism which, despite some inconsistencies, screens the more seriously alienated and disadvantaged into the system.

Second, the offender population and the corrections system are far from homogeneous. Offenders vary markedly in their commitment to crime, their demographic characteristics, and their potential as human resources. Prisons differ in their clientele and in their efforts toward its development and utilization. When addressing particular problems and programs, these variations are perhaps even more significant than the average characteristics of offenders and the corrections system.

Third, almost all offenders who are sent to jail are returned to society—a fact which is self-evident but all too often ignored. The corrections system is a transitory mechanism, a hiatus in the life of the typical offender. Whether it is beneficial or debilitating will affect not only the individual but society as a whole.

THE SORTING PROCESS

Only a small proportion of offenders "graduate" through the corrections system. Though documentation is difficult, evidence indicates that less than one-half of all offenses are reported; only a fifth of these are cleared by arrest; less than three-fourths of the adults and half of the juveniles who are arrested are convicted; and only a third of those convicted are sentenced to correctional institutions. To put it another way, for every hundred crimes, fifty are reported which lead to twelve arrests, six convictions, and two offenders being sent to jail.

There is a large element of chance in the "selection" of offenders at each level of the system, and yet there is also a basic equity. Among the many who commit crimes, some are caught the first time while others get away time after time; but probability is against the multiple offender. The odds are also against the offender who commits what are considered to be more serious crimes. For instance, the reported clearance rate on murders in 1969 was 86 percent compared with 11 percent for thefts of fifty dollars or less.[1] Thus, arrest tends to sort out and select the multiple offenders and those committing more serious crimes.

The selectivity process is much more complicated. The disposition of a case at each level depends on the strength of the evidence, the seriousness of the crime, the chances of rehabilitation, and to some unfortunate degree, the offender's influence and social standing. Prosecution will often be dropped against the person who can demonstrate a willingness to go straight or to make amends for his crimes. Those who cannot afford lawyers or cannot bring influence to bear may be more likely to be prosecuted, which tends, albeit unjustly, to screen in the more disadvantaged. In adult and juvenile courts, and in parole and probation hearings, those who are adjudged to have the least potential are retained in the corrections system while the others are released.

There are injustices at each of these judgmental levels, and decisions are not always made in the best interests of the offender and of society. Nevertheless, it is undoubtedly true—though impossible to document—that the system works in a general way to select those who are the "most criminal," those who have the most severe problems, and those who are the least rehabilitatable. Though there are some persons in prison who are no different than those on the street except that they got caught, the average offender tracked in the corrections system is extremely disadvantaged. And it is possible that his problems are more severe than his statistically measured characteristics would suggest. A matched group of disadvantaged prisoners and disadvantaged non-prisoners may well have different potentials if the corrections sorting mechanism works at all effectively. Whether or not this is true, the evidence is incontrovertible that an extremely hard-core group ends up in correctional institutions. [2]

THE HETEROGENEITY OF OFFENDERS

To claim that, on the average, offenders are extremely disadvantaged, and that the corrections system sorts out those who have the most severe problems does not mean that some number of these cannot be helped or that they will be more difficult to assist than similarly disadvantaged on the outside. Manpower services are never likely to reach all offenders; the question is whether there is a minority which can effectively be served, and how large this minority is. To answer this, the wide variations among individuals and institutions must be considered.

One of the most critical distinctions between individuals is age. There are obvious differences in the potential of a 40- to 50-year-old who has a long arrest and prison record and someone 15 or 16 who is brought in for his first offense. Of the more than 6 million arrests annually, roughly a fourth are persons under 18; and nearly two-fifths are persons under 21.[3] Recognizing the difference between younger and older offenders, separate court and institutional facilities have been established to deal with juveniles. The President's Commission on Law Enforcement and Administration of Justice found in 1966 there were 283,000 juveniles on parole and probation and 62,000 in institutions, compared with 534,000 adults on parole and probation and 343,000 in jail or prison. Obviously, young offenders are less likely to be institutionalized; and when they are, they serve shorter terms. The 1960 census found that less than a tenth of all jail or prison inmates were 19 years old or less, including a massively disproportionate number of nonwhites (Table 1).

Some distinction must also be made on the basis of criminal behavior. The actions and potential of narcotics addicts are typically different from those of car thieves or murderers, and it is reasonable to assume that they cannot all be helped in the same way and to the same extent. A number of different typological systems have been developed for classifying offenders; in some cases, these have been shown to have significant predictive value as well as use in program design. Employment problems of ex-prisoners vary with the number of prior commitments, with education, and with earlier employment success. These differences must be recognized in assessing the potential clientele for manpower services. The evidence indicates that the offender who is

8

Table 1. Average Population in Correctional Institutions, 1960

	Total	Federal and State Prisons and Reformatories	Local Jails and Work Houses
		All Races	
All ages	349,298	229,306	119,992
Male	332,952	220,765	112,187
Female	16,346	8,541	7,805
Under 15	736	137	599
15–19	32,379	19,815	12,564
20–24	65,906	44,803	21,103
25–39	156,236	108,093	48,143
40–59	82,955	50,123	32,832
60 and over	11,086	6,335	4,751
		Nonwhites	
All ages	133,249	87,401	45,848
Under 15	324	68	256
15–19	11,197	6,639	4,558
20–24	24,019	15,242	8,777
25–39	67,469	45,582	21,887
40–59	27,644	18,200	9,444
60 and over	2,596	1,670	926

SOURCE: U.S. Department of Commerce, Bureau of the Census, *U.S. Census of Population: 1960,* Series PC (2)-8A.

likely to do the best on his own is the better educated, married white with a stable employment history and no previous arrests, who is committed for a crime of violence. The least likely to succeed is the black narcotics addict who is young, single, and inexperienced in the world of work.[4] This does not mean, however, that resources should be concentrated on the former rather than the latter. It cannot be determined on a priori grounds whether the hardest core who need help most will benefit more or less than the offenders who are better off to begin with.

INSTITUTIONAL VARIATIONS

The impact of manpower services is also vitally affected by the variations in the institutional setting. There are essentially four penal systems: federal prisons, state prisons, local jails, and special juvenile facilities. In 1967 there were 19,600 in federal institutions and 175,300 in state prisons, with an annual turnover equal to about two-fifths of the total. In 1970 there were 160,863 in local jails, more than half of whom were awaiting arraignment or trial, with most of the remainder serving sentences of one year or less. Finally, there were more than 50,000 juveniles in special institutions in 1966, and 13,000 in the average in detention homes.[5]

These separate systems vary dramatically in their services to inmates. The juvenile facilities as a rule offer intensive assistance usually including medical care, education, and counseling. The 1965 average per capita cost for each juvenile was $3,411, almost double the expenditure in state prisons and more than three times that in local institutions. County and city jails do very little to rehabilitate or even maintain inmates. In 1966 only a tenth of jails were found to have educational facilities; only a seventh had recreation programs; and only a half offered medical care. The turnover in these facilities is high with an average stay of only a few months, and most are so small that institutional services are not feasible.[6]

The institutions most often considered as a potential manpower delivery agents are the federal and state systems, with their more than two hundred thousand inmates. There is a wide variation among states and within federal prisons in terms of the services which they now offer and their receptivity to new approaches. A survey of the 25 state prisons operating Manpower Development and Training Act (MDTA) training projects in 1968 and 1969 revealed that prior to instituting MDTA courses, ten offered no vocational training, five offered minimal training to less than 5 percent of the inmates, and only three had training programs in which more than 20 percent of the inmates participated. Likewise, in fifteen of the twenty-five, less than 20 percent of the prisoners received basic education.[7]

The picture is considerably better in the federal prisons. Most offer high school equivalency courses (GED) or other basic education, and most have training programs of some type. A 1964 survey of federal releases found that 35 percent had actually received training, with two-thirds of these participating for six months or more.[8] In terms of its manpower services, the average federal prison is probably more advanced than the average state institution, though some of the latter have developed highly innovative programs.

However, one of the most significant facts about the corrections system is that the largest proportion of offenders are not in institutions—they are on probation or parole. The United States has proportionately more people in jail than any other free industrial nation (200 per 100,000 compared to 59 for the United Kingdom, 73 for Denmark, and 153 for Finland).[9] Nevertheless, the number of convicted offenders outside of jail is more than twice the number inside; and the relative proportion is increasing rapidly. Community institutions, both public and private, must be used to reach these individuals.

Dealing with these disparate offender groups and consisting of a wide range of institutions which vary in their purpose and performance, the corrections "system" is more a patchwork than a coordinated processing mechanism to rehabilitated offenders. While efforts are needed to "systema-

11

tize" corrections, manpower programs in the conceivable future must be addressed to and tailored for specific offender groups and specific institutional levels.

CORRECTIONS AS A TRANSITIONAL MECHANISM

The basic idea behind corrections is to remove dangerous offenders from the community (or at least restrict their activities), to reform their attitudes, to improve their abilities, and to turn them loose as rehabilitated individuals who will not offend again and who will make a positive contribution to society. The employment problems of offenders, which will be subsequently documented, suggest that little is being done to increase their employability, while the large number who return to jail suggests that behavioral reform is also of little success. A six-year follow-up of persons released in 1963 found that six years later 65 percent had been rearrested. The very young and those who "get off" with their first offense are most likely to be rearrested, but all offender groups have a good chance of returning to crime (Chart 1).

Despite the failure of rehabilitative efforts, the fact remains that offenders are eventually turned back into the community as relatively free men. More than 100,000 leave federal and state prisons every year, and hundreds of thousands more pass through local jails. Even the most serious offenders are usually released. The average time served by those leaving federal institutions in 1970 was only 19.7 months with, for instance, kidnappers serving an average of only five years and robbers only four.[10]

Unless something positive is done during the relatively short period of public control, problems can only be complicated by incarceration. The prison environment, concentrating deprived and sometimes depraved individuals in a

CHART 1: PERCENT OF PERSONS REARRESTED WITHIN SIX YEARS

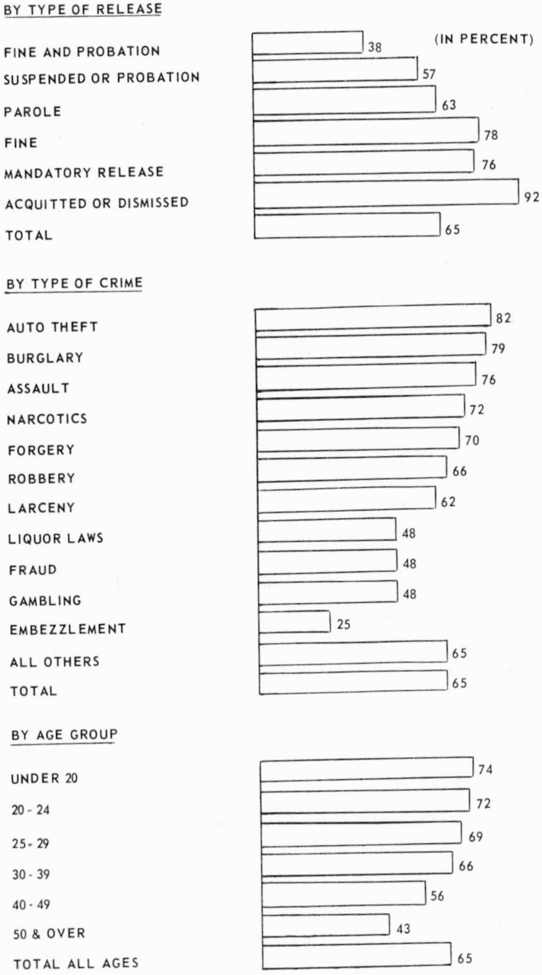

BY TYPE OF RELEASE

	(IN PERCENT)
FINE AND PROBATION	38
SUSPENDED OR PROBATION	57
PAROLE	63
FINE	78
MANDATORY RELEASE	76
ACQUITTED OR DISMISSED	92
TOTAL	65

BY TYPE OF CRIME

AUTO THEFT	82
BURGLARY	79
ASSAULT	76
NARCOTICS	72
FORGERY	70
ROBBERY	66
LARCENY	62
LIQUOR LAWS	48
FRAUD	48
GAMBLING	48
EMBEZZLEMENT	25
ALL OTHERS	65
TOTAL	65

BY AGE GROUP

UNDER 20	74
20 - 24	72
25 - 29	69
30 - 39	66
40 - 49	56
50 & OVER	43
TOTAL ALL AGES	65

SOURCE: Federal Bureau of Investigation, Uniform Crime Reports for the United States, 1969 (Washington, D.C.: U.S. Government Printing Office, 1970).

13

repressive atmosphere, may in itself have a debilitating effect. But institutionalization per se can be detrimental. Whether a person is in the military, in a hospital, or in prison, he suffers from the erosion of valuable skills, the loss of contacts and progress in the world of work, and the subsequent frictional difficulties of finding and settling down in a job. These transitional problems are compounded by the mark of Cain that is placed on the ex-offender, reducing his chances of successfully reintegrating into the community and especially of competing successfully in the labor market.

If the offender is to come out of prison with at least the same chances as he went in, efforts must be made to compensate for any deterioration of skills or attitudes; and transition mechanisms must be improved. The price of removing an individual from the community is not only the direct costs of food, shelter, and supervision, but also the indirect costs of underutilization and depreciation of human potential. In the case of offenders, these tend to be underutilized and underdeveloped to begin with. We must therefore run to even stay in place if we are to return individuals to society who are not worse off and more dangerous than when they first entered the system.

Employment Problems of Offenders

From the manpower perspective, the key variables to assess the development and utilization of human resources are those related to work. Poor education, undermotivation, the lack of skills, mental or physical deficiencies, and limited opportunities will be reflected in high unemployment, low wages, intermittent and low-status work patterns. Likewise, efforts to improve education, training, motivation, experience, and opportunities should result in improved employment patterns. These employment variables can be more easily and precisely measured than any others, and they are perhaps the most meaningful measures which can be derived.

Emphasis on employment rather than criminal behavior patterns is not unjustified. Work is perhaps the most important determinant of a successful adjustment to life. More than 95 percent of all prisoners are male, most of them in the prime working years between 18 and 45 when normally nine out of ten men are labor force participants devoting a major portion of their time and energies to work. For the adult male, work is one of the most important parts of life; and employment problems both reflect and cause difficulties elsewhere.

WORK VERSUS CRIME

Because of this obvious importance of a job and the equally obvious employment problems of offenders, a number of researchers have sought to demonstrate a cause and effect relationship. Received theory is that in a number of, though certainly not all, cases, the criminal turns to illicit activities because of his failure in work or his need for income. While few offenders are stealing bread to support their starving families, many have income or psychological "needs" which are not met through work. Crime offers a way of satisfying these.

The claim that employment problems are a major cause of crime is supported by a number of statistical studies. Glaser and Rice have found that property crimes by adults vary directly with the level of unemployment;[11] and Fleisher's complex statistical work supports this finding, though it suggests that the loss of income related to unemployment is more important than the actual loss of a job.[12] Other researchers have demonstrated that property crimes are much more likely to be committed by those in the lower socioeconomic classes,[13] while still others have shown that recidivism is significantly related to employment problems among parolees.[14]

Nevertheless, proving there is a *correlation* between unemployment and crime does not prove that there is a *cause and effect* relationship, nor does it prove that employment can be improved to a degree or at a cost which will make it an effective means of reducing illicit activity. It may well be that a "criminal mentality" or some nexus of behavioral traits (for instance, laziness) which cause criminality also lead to unemployment. There is convincing evidence that parolees with previously successful work experience are less likely to recidivate than their peers even if both are placed in the same kind of jobs with the same amount of training,[15] suggesting that jobs, skills, and earnings alone do not explain the degree of commitment to crime. Though the ex-offenders who are more successful in work are less likely to recidivate, there is no a priori reason to assume that if those doing worse in the labor market were trained and helped into the same jobs they would have equally low recidivism rates.

This is more than a nit-picking distinction. Employability may be improved without reducing the recidivism of offenders, or recidivism might be reduced without improving employability. Both are desirable goals, and each may be valued separately. The importance placed on each should influence the relative priority given to strategies which achieve different mixes of both at different costs.

From the manpower perspective, whether employment problems are a cause of crime and whether increased employability will reduce recidivism are secondary considerations. More significant is the fact that offenders are a group with serious employment problems. If these could be solved, or at least ameliorated, the individuals and society would benefit from the fuller use of the human resources whether or not the return to crime is forestalled. The questions then are how serious the problems of offenders are, and how easily they can be corrected by public efforts.

OFFENDERS AS A DISADVANTAGED GROUP

Offenders are drawn disproportionately from the ranks of the hard-core disadvantaged. Though statistics from the 1970 census are not yet available, the overwhelming evidence of earlier studies is that the average offender, particularly the one who is sent to prison, is a "loser" in the world of work. A comprehensive survey of releasees from federal prisons in 1964 found that 11 percent had never been employed and more than half had been employed a total of less than two years before incarceration even though their median age was 29, often because of earlier troubles with the law. Postrelease experiences were equally dismal. As of June 30, 1964, less than three-fifths were employed full time and 16 percent were unemployed. Comparative figures for the national male civilian labor force showed that four-fifths were employed full time and only 5 percent (or less than a third as many) were unemployed. Offenders are also drawn from and end up in the lowest paying jobs and lowest status occupations. The survey of federal releasees found that more than half had worked in unskilled or service jobs prior to commitment, and that more than two-fifths returned to such jobs upon release. The median monthly income of those employed was only $256[16] in 1964, when the average earnings of the private, nonagricultural sector were $394.

In interpreting these statistics, two points must be considered. First, the offender population is only a minority of a much larger group with severe employment problems; and

17

second, their removal from the labor market and their concommitant transitional difficulties complicate matters.

In concentrating on the employment problems of offenders, it is easy to lose sight of the fact that they are not the only ones with these problems, even if they are made more severe by incarceration or a criminal record. The 1964 data on federal releasees found that three out of five had completed less than a ninth-grade education, and only a fifth had completed high school. Of all men 18 years old and over in 1970, nearly 10 million had not completed ninth grade; and 18 million had not completed high school. A minority of these noninstitutionalized males with deficient educations, but not an insignificant number when compared to offenders, had severe employment problems. For instance, only seven out of ten of those with just eight years of schooling were labor force participants, as were only four out of five of those who had not completed high school, compared with 90 percent of those with a diploma. The males who had not finished high school were 50 percent more likely to be unemployed. Among those who worked, 29 percent of the ones not reaching high school and 21 percent of those not completing it were laborers and farm or service workers, compared with only 15 percent of all male high school graduates.[17]

These data can only be suggestive because good comparative statistics are unavailable, especially dealing with offenders who are not incarcerated. The indication, however, is that for every offender with employment problems, there are many nonoffenders in as bad shape. Even after the sorting process weeds out those with the most severe difficulties and they become concentrated in the prison system, there are still many nonoffenders who are no better off. A look at the characteristics of male enrollees in the Job Corps, MDTA, Operation Mainstream, the Concentrated Employment

Program (CEP), and other efforts for the disadvantaged suggests that there are hundreds of thousands of other "losers" who have motivational problems, low skills, educational deficiencies, and limited opportunities.

In trying to help overcome the employment problems of offenders—whether to reduce their recidivism or to tap their potential as a human resource—it is important to recognize their similarities with other hard-core unemployed. Criminal behavior tracks them into the corrections system, and it may indicate a different potential as a human resource; but as the boundaries between legal and illicit activities become obscured, especially in subcultures of crime, the distinction between the hard-core offender and the hard-core nonoffender becomes blurred.

One difference, however, is that when the offender gets tracked in the corrections system, his job difficulties automatically intensify. Much has been made of the high level of unemployment among Vietnam veterans, though in fact it was only a fifth higher than for nonveterans of the same age in 1970. Any time an individual is removed from the labor force and his skills are applied to tasks with little carry-over into civilian use, he will have transitional difficulties. Likewise, being in jail or prison creates frictional adjustment problems. And while the veteran is helped in his transition by special government efforts and favorable public attitudes, the offender is handicapped by constricting laws and negative public opinion.

Another difference between the offender and the nonoffender is that much greater control can be exerted when a person has violated the law. In some ways this complicates matters since the need for protecting society or punishing the individual may run contrary to the needs of the offender. In other ways it can potentially make things easier because the individual can be coerced into doing things he might not otherwise do which are for his own benefit. But this difference should not be exaggerated. The environment and values of the average offender are probably not much different than that of the average disadvantaged person, and the social control which is exercised, at least outside of prisons and jails, may be more form than substance.

THE MANPOWER APPROACH

If offenders are then viewed as another hard-core group, whose problems are accentuated but not fundamentally altered by their contact with the corrections system, manpower strategies and methodologies not so different from those already used for other disadvantaged groups may have applicability.

Experience with manpower programs over the last decade has shown that a variety of services are often needed to help those with the most serious problems. These services include work orientation, vocational guidance, skill training, remedial education, health care, counseling, placement, job development, and income maintenance. The proper mix in any particular case depends on the individual and the institutional circumstances, but all may be required. And experience has also shown that even with all these services, only modest average gains can be expected in dealing with the hardest core. Overcoming the multiple deficiencies in the individual and the debilitating influences of his environment takes a great deal of time and effort. However, there is fairly conclusive evidence that *some* strategies can serve *some* hard-core groups with *some* degree of success. The goal of manpower policy has been to improve the employment experience of those who are helped. Unemployment rate changes, wage gains, occupational redistributions, and other work-related improvements have been the basic criteria for measuring performance; and on these grounds, modest success has been demonstrated. Efforts have been made, at least in a crude way, to allocate resources on the basis of such demonstrated contributions to employability. The basic thrust of manpower methodology is that program impact can be and must be demonstrated in a concrete fashion. In considering the extension of manpower services to offenders, the same approach should be used.

Since offenders are only one among many groups who need help in overcoming their employment problems and since the resources available for remedial education and manpower services are limited and can reach only a small portion of the potential universe of need, manpower efforts must be directed where they will do the most good. Severity of need, "worthiness," and spillover impacts must all be considered; but the effectiveness of assistance programs must also be a prime criterion. Resources must be allocated on the basis of the relative costs and benefits of providing services in different ways to the different groups. If more efforts are to be exerted on behalf of offenders, it must be demonstrated that the individuals are amenable to development, that the institutional setting can be utilized, and that employability can be improved. Equally important, it must be demonstrated that these goals can be achieved as effectively for offenders as for other disadvantaged groups.

Services for Offenders

A priori reasoning cannot determine the effectiveness of manpower services for offenders, but it can suggest some of the characteristics of the institutional setting and the offender population which will contribute to success or failure.

There are obvious impediments to helping offenders. One is that manpower and rehabilitative services are not always adaptable to the punishment and detention functions of the corrections system. Most persons would rather be out of prison than in, or off parole than on; safeguards are necessary to assure that sentences are served, or at least are shortened by society's rather than the individual's decision. Though these should be minimized where possible, it is a fact of life that many among the offender population are dangerous to society; and to control this dangerous minority, it may be necessary to control them all. The predominant concerns of most penal personnel have been detention and punishment before rehabilitation; and though the latter function may be given increased emphasis, the former will remain important. Manpower efforts will still have to be adjusted to a time framework where sentences are primarily related to the severity of the crime. Prisons and prisoners will continue to be isolated geographically unless or until new community institutions are built; this makes it difficult to provide the needed services. Strict discipline will necessarily be maintained, with an emphasis on minimizing the costs and maximizing the security of detention. These constraints may hamper the effectiveness of manpower services relative to those provided to nonoffenders.

Another impediment is the offender population itself. Individually, the fact that offenders committed crimes may indicate motivational, emotional, or mental problems which are more serious than for other disadvantaged persons. The fact that some are caught for crimes which are being committed by others who are not caught does not change the fact that the average offender is more "criminal" than the average person with severe employment problems. Whether or not this is a major impediment is difficult to say. With limited resources, manpower services will be available for only a minority; and it may be possible to find a substantial number of offenders who are not poorly motivated. On the other hand, the criminal subculture which exists in prisons and jails, as a result of throwing together hardened criminals with those who could otherwise be salvaged, may mean that promising individuals cannot be effectively singled out for attention. For instance, the prisoner or offender subculture may work against participation and achievement in training programs.

There are also, however, some factors which could contribute to the success of manpower and remedial education services. Most significant of these is the control which society has over the individual, at least while he is in prison or jail. This can be exercised to insure participation in development services. For instance, high dropout rates have undermined the effectiveness of many vocational training programs; but this is unlikely to be much of a problem in prisons. Probation and parole can also be used in a discretionary way, basing continued freedom on successful performance in manpower programs. Income supplements and money incentives are not as critical in a prison setting, greatly reducing the cost of services. At the same time, subsistence, health care, and recreation are provided to some degree as a part of incarceration so that manpower and remedial education resources do not have to be used for these ends.

There is no way to balance these conceptual pros and cons. The only way to assess the chances of improving employability is to look carefully at past experience with remedial education and manpower services for offenders, and especially the experimental and demonstration projects initiated to test their impact.

PRESENT EFFECTIVENESS

In recent years some important first steps have been taken within the corrections system to help offenders overcome their employment problems, but their aggregate impact to date has been minimal. Persons on probation and parole or awaiting trial may get help from general manpower programs, such as CEP or Job Opportunities in the Business Sector (JOBS) programs; they may be placed and counseled by the Employment Service (ES); or they might get special attention in half-way houses. Nevertheless, the opportunities for such assistance are limited; and the overwhelming majority of offenders outside of state and federal prisons receive no special help in preparing for and finding jobs.

The burden for education, training, and rehabilitation has fallen mainly to the prison system. Experience has shown that it has been largely unsuccessful in this mission. As indicated, less than one out of twenty state prisoners receives training and only one out of five receives any basic education. Though a larger share of federal inmates receives vocational training, this may consist largely of work in prison industries, which teaches few transferable skills. In the last three years, more intensive services have been provided under MDTA, reaching around 5,000 prisoners of state and federal institutions in 1971; but other vocational training has not amounted to much or at least has not had much impact. For instance, a survey of the employment experience of federal releasees in June 1964 revealed that those who had received some vocational training did no better than those who had not, unless they received it for an extensive period (Table 2).

This experience, however, offers little indication of the feasibility of vocational training. It simply attests to the low level of priority and resources devoted to such aims in the past. Altogether, less than 7 percent of the 121,163 persons employed in correctional agencies in 1966 were counselors, teachers, chaplains, and clinicians, or their supervisors. This amounted to about one staff person devoted to any aspect of rehabilitation for every 150 offenders.[18] Besides having

Table 2. **Employment Status of Federal Parolees and Mandatory Releasees by Vocational Training in Prison, June 1964**

	No Vocational Training	Vocational Training	1 Year or More Vocational Training
Employed	83.3	83.5	88.6
Full time	62.6	61.7	60.0
Part time	19.6	20.1	24.3
Unknown	1.1	1.7	4.3
Unemployed	16.7	16.5	11.4

SOURCE: George Pownall, "Employment Problems of Released Prisoners," mimeographed (University of Maryland, College Park, Md., 1969), p. 106.

limited resources, the internal vocational training efforts have not been designed to test or improve the effectiveness of services. Data were usually not gathered and little effort was devoted to measuring their impact.

INNOVATIVE PROGRAMS FOR OFFENDERS

Though operational efforts are still limited, research into the employment problems of offenders and the manpower aspects of corrections has expanded dramatically in the last few years. Beginning in the middle sixties, a number of experimental and demonstration projects were initiated to test specific concepts and approaches. These were funded by a variety of federal agencies including the Bureau of Prisons, the Law Enforcement Assistance Administration (LEAA), the Social and Rehabilitation Service (the vocational rehabilitation agency), the National Institute of Mental Health, the District of Columbia Department of Corrections, and the Manpower Administration of the Department of Labor. A Justice Department survey in August 1971 estimated that these various agencies were spending over $11 million on specifically research-oriented activities, and many millions more on operational efforts of an experimental nature.[19]

25

Many of the funded research projects have manpower implications, whether or not this is their prime focus. The Bureau of Prisons is studying, among other things, work release, adult basic education, testing procedures for assignment to prison jobs, incentive pay experiments, and several vocational programs. The LEAA is sponsoring research on pretrial release, probation subsidies, and the effectiveness of community-based corrections. The Social and Rehabilitation Service has funded studies of a number of vocational rehabilitation projects and approaches while the District of Columbia has studied work release, half-way houses, and other community treatment facilities.

Most significant, however, are the burgeoning efforts of the Department of Labor. In fiscal 1971 it accounted for $4.7 million of the $11 million spent by federal agencies for research, with the overwhelming majority of the funds going to study manpower problems and programs. Among the wide range of subjects being studied are social reinforcement in prison manpower programs, fidelity bonding for ex-offenders, income and placement assistance, communication between parole authorities and prisoner training programs, work release laws, and discrimination against ex-offenders in public employment.

As a result of previous experimental and demonstration projects, offender manpower programs are also beginning to be implemented on an operational basis. In fiscal 1971, $13.7 million was spent for operational programs in addition to the research and development monies. It is projected that in fiscal 1972, *total* expenditures for offenders by the Department of Labor will amount to $29.4 million, a dramatic increase from the $6.2 million level of fiscal 1970. This will include $5.3 million for research and experimentation, $12 million for the implementation of five state comprehensive correctional manpower models, $1.5 million for special employment services, and $10 million in state matching funds for vocational training in prisons.[20]

FROM THE EXPERIMENTAL TO THE OPERATIONAL

The Department of Labor has been able to expand some of its experimental and demonstration (E&D) projects into operational programs for offenders within its broad mandate under the Manpower Development and Training Act. There are limits, however, to the number of dollars which can be reallocated administratively without legislative authorization. We are now nearing a juncture where legislation is needed to specifically articulate policies for offenders.

A number of bills are pending which, at least in part, are addressed to the employment problems of offenders. Many of these seek to break down specific barriers to employment through the expungement of criminal records, changes in civil service regulations, and the opening of public jobs. Most envision manpower programs as a vital part of total institutional change. For instance, the Omnibus Correctional Reform Act of 1971, introduced by Senator Bayh, would reserve 40 percent of LEAA monies for the creation of community-centered institutions and other reforms. Training, job placement, counseling, and other manpower services for offenders would receive $400 million over the next four years, and prison education programs would also be subsidized.

Another approach is to authorize expanded services for offenders as a separate manpower bill. Senator Javits and Congressman Esch have introduced the Comprehensive Correctional Employment and Training Act which authorizes $40 million in fiscal 1972, $100 million in fiscal 1973, and $200 million in fiscal 1974 to provide a wide range of manpower services. These funds would come on top of those already being expended. They would be administered by the Secretary of Labor who would be able to contract with any public or private group to carry out these programs, providing funds could provide leverage for the coordination of other programs.

A number of specific strategies are authorized: (1) pretrial intervention in which offenders would be offered manpower training and other assistance prior to the disposition of their cases; (2) vocational training and basic education programs in prison; (3) subsidies and services for off-site work experience and prerelease; (4) income maintenance during prison training and upon release to ease the transition back into the labor market; (5) bonding assistance as surety for financial loss to employers of offenders; (6) opening of the existing manpower programs to ex-offenders either on probation, parole, or free in the community; (7) special funding for employment services to beef up their assistance to offenders, both in prison and in the community; and (8) efforts to eliminate artificial barriers to employment, along with creation of special jobs for offenders in corrections.

The thrust of this bill and other pending legislation is to provide a comprehensive "shopping list" of strategies and increased funding to implement them. There is no articulation of priorities among the alternatives, and the Secretary of Labor would be left with broad discretion. The Javits-Esch bill authorizes a thorough study "to identify the appropriate stages in the corrections process during which a criminal offender can benefit most effectively from participation in manpower training and employment programs." This would provide some guidance to decisionmakers in setting priorities and choosing among alternative strategies. More likely, however, a shotgun approach would be used, funding a little of everything until more concrete evidence of success or failure could be gathered.

Nevertheless, much of the groundwork has already been laid in the experimental and demonstration projects of the Department of Labor and other agencies. Even though these have been limited in scale and duration, a conscious effort has been made to try out new approaches and in some cases to measure their success or failure. These have been undertaken at all levels in the corrections system, from pretrial to postrelease, and they have experimented with affording a wide variety of services to offenders. Though evidence is limited on these projects and the different approaches are often interdependent, an examination of the separate services at each level of intervention can provide the basis for working hypotheses and can suggest, in at least the broadest terms, where and to what extent resources should be allocated to manpower efforts for offenders.

Alternatives to Incarceration

Evidence indicates that incarceration only increases the employment and other problems of most offenders. Even if improvements could be made, the fact remains that some offenders who now are sent to jail for lack of an alternative do not need institutionalization to be rehabilitated. They would benefit more from remaining in the community under some system of public guidance and assistance. Prison maintenance is costly, and society as well as the individual would benefit if offenders could be reintegrated successfully without incarceration.

Recognizing these savings and the inadequacy and overcrowded conditions in most jails, the courts have made increasing use of probation, especially in dealing with juvenile offenders. The President's Commission on Law Enforcement and Administration of Justice estimated that slightly over half of the offenders sentenced to correctional treatment are now on probation, and that the number of probationers will increase at two and one-half times the institutional and parole populations. By 1975 it is estimated that there will be over 1 million offenders on probation with only 770,000 on parole or in institutions.[21]

This increasing reliance on probation puts pressure on the probation system, which must not only help those who are committed to its care but must usually also prepare pre-sentencing materials for judges. As of 1965, the average caseload for adult probation officers was over a hundred; while for juvenile officers, it was around 75.[22] This provides little opportunity for individual attention or intensive services. Many offenders are simply turned back into the community without the assistance they need, while a much smaller but still significant number that could be diverted with a little help are sent on to prisons.

Employment services, in particular, may be needed by these offenders. To test this, several experimental and demonstration projects have been initiated to intervene prior to the offender's trial, finding him a job or training and, if successful, using the experience as a grounds for dismissal or probation rather than institutionalization. A few projects have also been oriented to helping probationers, often in special institutional settings. Lessons can be learned from these efforts, though they are far from conclusive.

PRETRIAL INTERVENTION

The Manhattan Court Employment Project, operated in New York City by the Vera Institute of Justice, and Project

Crossroads, operated in Washington, D.C. by the National Committee for Children and Youth, provide employment-oriented services to young men and women in the pretrial stage of the criminal process, concentrating on those brought in for their first offense. The courts suspend judgment for three months in the cases of participants and agree to consider dropping charges upon successful completion of the project.

Despite very extensive "creaming," both projects work with a very disadvantaged clientele. On the average, the screeners in the Manhattan project examine a thousand cases to come up with only ten participants. To be eligible, the offender has to be a male resident of New York City between 16 and 45 years old; he must be unemployed or earning no more than $125 a week; he cannot be a drug addict, be charged with homicide, rape, or assault, or have previously served more than a year in prison. About nine out of ten cases are eliminated on these bases, and the final choices are made by personal interviews aimed at determining abilities and motivation.

Nevertheless, the selected clientele has many handicaps. Of the 850 participants in the first 23 months of the project, half were black and a third Puerto Rican; the average had a tenth-grade education and was 21 years old; all had employ-ment problems of one sort or another. Despite intensive efforts to screen out narcotics addicts, almost a fourth of all participants later proved to have a dependence on drugs which interfered with their participation.

The chief emphasis of the Manhattan project is on inten-sive group counseling, job development, and placement. Participants are assigned to counselors (who are sometimes ex-offenders themselves) in caseloads of 20 to 25 and group sessions are used to augment individual attention. On the basis of the counselor's determinations of employability and

31

on the availability of developed jobs, placements are made. Most of these are in low-level service or factory jobs with no potential for upgrading, but the average salary in 1969 was $83 a week. Since no one earning over $70 a week was initially accepted into the project, this represented some improvement. Of the first 850 participants, 463 were referred to employment or training at least once, and of these, 309 were placed. More than half of the referrals were sent to two or more employers, and a third of the placements had to be placed two or more times. Apparently, in a large number of cases, these disadvantaged offenders did not live up to employer expectations or else they were dissatisfied with the jobs they got. Despite the intensive placement activities, a follow-up study found that that more than half of the former participants were unemployed or else their employment status was unknown, which suggests that the services could not have had a very significant impact.[23] Some very crude cost-benefit calculations have been done on the basis of before and after data on wages; these purport to show substantial earnings gains which far outweigh the project costs ($1,500 per successful completer). But the data are so sketchy and the assumptions so questionable that no judgments can be made other than the self-evident conclusion that when jobs are found for the previously unemployed, wages will improve.[24] Needless to say, jobs are much more difficult to find in the current economic climate, and placements and wage gains have declined precipitously according to project statistics.

There is some evidence of a favorable impact on recidivism. Between April 1967 and October 1968, only 32 percent of participants compared with 46 percent of a control group were rearrested.[25] It is not known, however, how much of this difference is explained by the creaming of the experimental group or by the supervision provided under the program as opposed to its manpower services. There is also some less favorable evidence. An eighth of the participants were rearrested even before they completed the project. Drug users, in particular, failed to benefit. More than three-fourths were terminated from the project compared to only two-fifths of nonusers, and their chances of being rearrested were markedly higher. Nevertheless, on the basis of its crudely supported claims of success, the Manhattan project has been expanded and extended to other areas in New York City. Improvements are reportedly being made in its procedures and its impact.

Project Crossroads in Washington, D.C., did a much better job of measuring performance, though not necessarily of assisting participants. Its extensive follow-up and carefully selected control group have facilitated more rigorous analysis of its performance.

Like the Manhattan project, Crossroads provided counseling, job development, and placement services to a very disadvantaged clientele: 84 percent were male; 87 percent, nonwhite; three-fifths, 18 and 19 years old; 63 percent had less than a high school education; less than half were employed at the time of intake; and most of these earned less than $1.75 per hour at unskilled jobs.

Despite these handicaps, participants benefited somewhat in their employment status, their wages, and their occupational distribution. For instance, 44 percent of a sample of participants had an average wage of $2.00 or more per hour one year after the project compared with 20 percent at intake (though some of this gain is due to aging). In the year prior to the project, 30 percent worked at least 80 percent of the year; but in the year following, nearly half worked this consistently. Where 62 percent were unskilled workers at intake, only half were in this category after the project. Recidivism was also reduced, though the benefits diminished after the project was over. Only 29 percent recidivated during the three months of the project compared with 50 percent of controls; but 71 percent recidivated during the following eleven months compared with only 50 percent of controls.[26]

Overall, the impact of the program on employability and recidivism was statistically significant but not very glamorous when compared with a control group. An extremely careful and complex cost-benefit analysis which weighed the $200 enrollee cost per month against employment gains as well as against estimated reductions in court expenses and costs of crime found that the project was "worthwhile," with a benefit-cost ratio between 1.8 and 2.2.[27] While there was nothing wrong with the methodology, the benefit calculations were extremely inclusive, projecting extensive savings in court and corrections costs far into the future; and the resulting ratio is larger than would have been the case if other assumptions had been used. Nevertheless, it is interesting that almost the same ratio of benefits to costs was found in an analysis of the Job Corps impact.[28] This suggests that programs for a disadvantaged clientele of this age, while they are worthwhile, have only a modest impact, and that not too much should be expected from offender programs which serve this group.

The most basic lesson from Crossroads was that performance could be improved by concentrating services on a more selective group, specifically, married males in their early twenties who had previously been employed. It was demonstrated that few teenagers would benefit from these pretrial employment services. A juvenile program was begun in the fall of 1969, and though no good data are available as yet, indications are that it had little impact on employment or recidivism. Under the adult program which has been discussed, 18- and 19-year-olds were more likely to be unfavorably terminated from the program and more likely to recidivate than older participants.[29]

Although the evidence is crude, the Manhattan and Crossroads projects demonstrate that pretrial manpower programs can help offenders by marginally improving their employment and diverting them from jail; society benefits to the degree that the increased output and reduced corrections expenses seem to outweigh the costs of the program. On the basis of this evidence, modest expansion is warranted to test out the concept more fully. Actions have already been taken in this direction. The budget for the Manhattan project has been picked up by New York City, and its method has been applied in other boroughs. The Manpower Administration is now funding pretrial programs in Atlanta, Baltimore, Boston, San Francisco, Cleveland, Minneapolis, and San Antonio.[30] However, given the enthusiasm for any approach which offers an alternative to incarceration, there is a danger that pretrial efforts will be further expanded before their effectiveness is carefully analyzed and their design improved. The experience of the Manhattan and Crossroads projects alone does not justify the massive implementation of this approach, though it does offer some hope that this strategy may eventually prove to be effective.

COMMUNITY TREATMENT

The central thrust of "advanced" correctional thinking is to provide community treatment as an alternative to institutionalization. In response to the increasing use of probation in recent years, there has been a rapid proliferation of intervention programs aimed at probationers. One approach is to intensify regular probation services, reduce caseloads, and in some cases add specialists, including manpower personnel.

Another approach is nonresidential treatment, for instance, using guided group interaction in a daytime program which includes employment, counseling, and other assistance, as was done in the much copied Provo and Essexfields experiments. A third approach, sometimes difficult to distinguish from institutionalization, is intensive residential treatment, in which offenders are assigned to live in special community facilities outside regular prisons and jails.

Despite the attention these strategies have received and their expanded implementation, they remain grossly inadequate relative to the rapidly growing number of probationers. More than this, it has yet to be proved in any rigorous way that they are more effective at rehabilitating an offender than incarceration (though usually they are found to be cheaper). For instance, experiments with "probation plus" have shown that merely reducing probation officers' caseloads does not increase the officers' effectiveness.[31] Apparently more effective are intensified services to selected groups.

Perhaps the most successful probation program has been the Community Treatment Project (CTP), initiated in 1961 in California and now operating in a number of locations. Emphasis in this project is placed on intensive counseling, though basic education, half-way house residence, and placement are also given to some participants. The most innovative feature has been the extensive use of a typological classification system in assigning participants to probation officers and to other activities. Follow-up data suggest that this increases the effectiveness of the services. Between 1961 and 1968 only 31 percent of CTP participants had violated parole or were arrested within 15 months compared to 50 percent of controls. A number of separate cohort analyses support the finding of a very significant difference in recidivism resulting from classification.[32]

Yet such evidence is far from conclusive. A careful study of the Community Treatment Project has suggested that its apparently positive impact was to a large extent the result of the favorable treatment given to participants relative to other offenders violating the terms of probation or parole. For instance, 68 percent of control failures in 1966 but only 29 percent of experimental failures were accounted for by agents' recommendations that parole be revoked. When the offense is of low or moderate severity, experimentals are less likely to have their parole revoked; and they thus have a lower recidivism rate.[33] Differential treatment of this sort is a possibility in any program where there is interaction between administrators and those with authority over the individual; for instance, it might be an explanation for some of the reduced recidivism noted in pretrial projects.

Whatever the success or failure of these community treatment approaches for probationers, the fact remains that manpower services have not played a significant role. Manpower policymakers must resist the temptation to jump on the bandwagon by assuming, without proof, that more offenders should be diverted from prisons and treated in the community. There is not yet any evidence whether adults can better be served in this way or, if so, whether placement, counseling, and training can have a favorable impact.

SERVING THE STOCK RATHER THAN DIVERTING THE FLOW

Rather than initiating manpower programs as an alternative to incarceration, which will divert more offenders from prisons and jails, it might be better to serve those who are already on probation. Despite the recent proliferation of community-based institutions to which offenders can be assigned during probation, services remain grossly inadequate.

Most probationers are left to their own devices in solving their employment problems. The court sets certain standards and regulations for behavior, and probation officers may set others, but rarely are they concerned with increasing employability. The ever-increasing number of probationers receive almost no assistance despite the fact that their problems are severe and their recidivism rates are high. Since probationers can utilize existing institutions in their community, and the court can require their participation, logic demands that efforts be made to insure probationers' access to the existing manpower system. This means opening any closed doors within this system—for instance, eliminating any restrictions against training or placing those with criminal records—and reaching out to serve them. One-stop individualized services are probably needed to augment other probation treatment, whether offered by ad hoc community groups, the parole office staff, vocational rehabilitation personnel, the Employment Service, or delivery agents such as CEP's or Community Action Agencies (CAA's).

If the lessons learned from the pretrial experiments can be carried over, efforts should concentrate on the more mature and work-oriented offenders, though no one should be denied the help of manpower programs if he wants it. Large-scale experiments are needed to test the effectiveness and methods of delivering manpower services to probationers, and every effort must be made to break down any barriers which may exist for them within the system. As an example, offender quotas or goals might be set under the manpower programs, with increased funds allocated specifically for these purposes. Efforts must also be made to determine how well offenders have done and are doing in these programs. This requires careful experimentation rather than immediate, large-scale implementation.

Vocational Training in Prisons

Though many offenders may be diverted from prison by manpower services, there is little likelihood in the immediate future that resources will be adequate to do more than check further growth of the institutional population. Something must be done for those who are now and will in the future be removed from the community. One possibility is vocational training in prison.

One of the most basic employment problems of the incarcerated offender is that he lacks the qualities and skills demanded in the marketplace. Usually a failure in school, he is unlikely to have had any vocational training or to have benefited if he did. Working in a number of jobs or not at all, he has acquired few skills and many bad work habits. Vocational training, combined with counseling, basic education, and other related services, may be needed if he is to find and hold a higher paying job.

Institutional vocational training has been provided on a large scale to the disadvantaged throughout the nation since 1962 under the Manpower Development and Training Act. In fiscal 1970 there were 140,000 MDTA (institutional) enrollees who were provided a combination of manpower services built around specific vocational training in special skill centers and in courses given in the schools. Experience has demonstrated that this institutional training can significantly increase the earnings and reduce the unemployment of disadvantaged workers—many of whom have employment problems as severe as offenders.[34] The question is whether the MDTA institutional training approach can be effectively applied in a prison setting and, if so, whether resources should be allocated to this effort on a large scale.

39

OFFENDERS UNDER MDTA

There is a good deal of experience on which this judgment can rest. With MDTA experimentation and demonstration funds, a number of projects have been carried out to test the effectiveness of combinations of vocational training and remedial education in the prison setting combined with post-release supportive services. These include Project First Chance at the South Carolina Correctional Institute; Project Challenge in Lorton, Virginia; Project Fresh Start in Detroit, Michigan; the Draper Project in Elmore, Alabama; and the Rikers Island Project in New York. All of these efforts claimed to have a positive impact on the employability of offenders. However, only in the case of the Rikers Island Project was there a careful selection of a control group and a rigorous analysis of results. Comparison of the postrelease experience of participants and controls led to the conclusion that this approach could be highly effective:

A program of vocational education and training in a jail, coupled with appropriate post-release services to manage re-entry into free society, *does* make a difference in subsequent job performance and social adjustment of young offenders. Contrary to traditional expectations, and though the jail is a short-term institution with consequently brief periods of inmate availability for training, enough time is available to initiate a sequence of activity which can have significant rehabilitative impact. A constructive program can be established to wisely use the time inmates spend in jail.[35]

Based largely on the evidence of success at Rikers Island and also on the favorable claims of other pilot projects, Congress amended the Manpower Development and Training Act in 1966, adding Section 251 which gave the secretary of labor operational authority to initiate MDTA projects on a larger scale in prisons through June 30, 1970. More than fifty projects were funded under 251, but the authority was not extended in 1970. A few projects continue to receive MDTA monies out of general-purpose allocations, but most are now operated from state matching funds. There are presently an estimated 55 projects with some 5,000 inmate trainees.[36]

Despite the expansion of these training programs, there is limited evidence of their effectiveness. A careful study of 25 individual projects funded from 1968 through mid-1969 revealed that they had a very negligible impact on the post-release employment experience of participants.[37]

In part, the greater success of the Rikers Island and other demonstration projects resulted from their intensive, experimental nature. It is often the case that projects successful on a limited scale cannot be expanded effectively. The extent of and ingredients for the success of Rikers Island must be carefully analyzed to assess its replicability, while the limitations revealed by the more extensive efforts under 251 must be examined to see if they can be overcome.

THE RIKERS ISLAND PROJECT

The Rikers Island Project began in 1963 as a joint effort of the City College of New York and the New York City Department of Corrections, with funding from the Department of Labor's Manpower Administration. After some initial difficulties, the City College's role was taken over by the Staten Island Mental Health Society, which directed the project to its completion in 1967.

The main thrust of the Rikers Island effort was to provide vocational training to a sample of young men in the New York City jail and to study their postrelease experience. Out of the three thousand 16- to 21-year-old males committed to the Rikers Island jail between December 1963 and June 1965, 264 were selected on the basis of skills and educational tests. Of these, 137 were given training on IBM punched-card data processing machines, as well as remedial reading help, counseling, rather extensive job placement assistance, and some cash upon release. The remaining 127 were given no special assistance and served as a control group.

Beginning in March 1966, efforts were made to measure and compare the experiences of these two groups. There were several indications from these that the vocational training and related services had helped the individuals.

First, since their release, only 48 percent of the experimental group had committed crimes which returned them to jail or prison, compared with 66 percent of controls.

Second, only 54 percent of the drug addicts in the experimental group returned to jail, compared with 80 percent of those in the controls.

Third, 48 percent of experimentals ended up in white-collar jobs and only 5 percent worked at physical labor, compared with only 18 and 22 percent respectively for controls.

Fourth, 25 percent of the jobs held by experimentals usually led to promotion, compared with only 3 percent of those held by controls.[38]

Thus, participation in the Rikers Island Project seemed to aid these young offenders. Recidivism was reduced even for narcotics addicts, and more attractive jobs were secured.

However, there are a number of caveats about these conclusions, which were recognized by the project directors, but were often forgotten by those who publicized the project's success. There are problems in any social experiment in picking a comparable control group. In this case, the experimentals and controls matched up very well on almost every social and economic variable except one—drug use. Out of the experimental group, only 13 percent reported the use of heroin, morphine, or cocaine, compared with 38 percent of the controls. Recidivism among drug-using controls was 80 percent, compared with 54 percent for those not reporting drug use.[39] If controls had had the same proportion of users as experimentals, their overall recidivism rate would have been lower. In addition, a much higher proportion of drug-using controls than drug-using experimentals reported daily use before incarceration, suggesting that the controls were much farther down the road to addiction and much less likely to be helped by training and other services.

The greater incidence of serious addiction among controls also explains many of the postrelease employment differentials. According to project reports, 12 percent of controls never worked or were unable to work after release, compared with only 2 percent of the experimental group; 15 percent rated their employment experience as overwhelmingly negative. And yet the proportion who succeeded was roughly the same for both groups; for instance, 42 percent of controls rated their employment experience strongly positive compared with only 33 percent of experimentals. Evidence from a variety of sources suggests that employment problems are worse for addicts; and if they had not been overrepresented, the portion of control failures might have been no larger than that of experimentals.[40]

Another revealing fact is that according to employers' ratings, only 29 percent of the experimental group were hired for work even indirectly related to their IBM training and only 18 percent specifically for such jobs.[41] Placement was difficult in keypunch jobs because employers did not want to have offenders working next to women, who predominate in this occupation. Since controls matched the experimental group in most demographic attributes and since for most experimentals their skills were not used, it must be assumed that their greater penetration of white-collar jobs was largely the result of placement efforts rather than vocational training per se.

These arguments do not mean that the Rikers Island project was not useful. It was, after all, an experiment to see whether or not vocational training and other services could help young offenders. And there is no doubt that it had a favorable impact on the postrelease employment experience and the recidivism of participants. On the other hand, this impact should not be exaggerated. It is marginal at best, and there are real doubts that vocational training per se made much of a contribution.

Whatever its impact, there are questions about the replicability of the Rikers Island experience. For one thing, excellent leadership was provided for the project. Without it, any success would have been unlikely; and it is extremely doubtful that it can be duplicated on a large scale. On the other hand, the Rikers Island Project provided training in keypunch operation only to find later that, because of the large numbers of women in this work, employers were more reluctant than usual to hire young male offenders. Other courses of instruction may have been more successful, and other age groups of offenders may have done better (or worse).

THE "251" PROJECTS

The projects funded under Section 251 of the Manpower Development and Training Act provide a much better basis for assessing the effectiveness of vocational training in prisons. Twenty-five projects (in 30 institutions) funded in 1968–69 have been carefully studied. These provided assistance to 2,877 offenders, all but 184 of them in state prisons, with a high concentration in the South. The clientele was almost totally male and two-fifths nonwhite, with more than three-fifths between 20 and 29 years old, and only 10 percent under 20. It was obviously "creamed" from the total prison population since seven out of ten had nine or more years of education, compared with only two-fifths of the national inmate population of state prisons.[42] Nevertheless, these trainees were significantly more disadvantaged than the national MDTA clientele, of which four out of five had more than eight years of schooling in 1968 and two out of five had completed high school, compared with less than a fourth of prison participants.[43]

The vocation of training and its intensity varied markedly from project to project. Most participants were given welding, auto mechanics, and upholstery courses, but over thirty different fields were offered. The average cost per trainee was between $1,000 and $1,500, of which between a fifth and a fourth went for payments to trainees. Vocational courses varied widely in their quality, with more than a third (in the judgment of field investigators) having serious equipment problems or other deficiencies. The claim made by those who have evaluated the program is that the uninspired selection of courses and the poor way they were implemented by many prison staffs undermined the effect they could have had with more careful and innovative selection and implementation.

A number of supportive services were provided in addition to vocational training. Four-fifths of enrollees received basic education, and nine-tenths received counseling; but again, the quality and duration of these services varied markedly. More than half of the trainees received special job development and placement assistance from either the Employment Service or the MDTA staff,[44] but many received no special help.

To assess the impact of these services, the postrelease experiences of enrollees and over 1,000 controls were measured three and six months after release. There are some very technical reservations about the analytic methods and the data base; but despite these deficiencies, the evidence is more comprehensive than for any other offender manpower effort.[45] The groups of experimentals and controls were matched according to most variables, with the exceptions that 49.4 percent of controls were 24 years old or less, compared with only 38.3 percent of trainees; and that only 34.3 percent had three to nine years of previous gainful employment, compared with 42.3 percent of trainees. There was no correction for these possible causes of less successful postrelease adjustment by controls. On the other hand, the nonresponse bias probably worked in favor of controls since closer tabs were kept on trainees and failures at work among controls were probably less likely to respond.

At any rate, the follow-up data suggest that training and other services had little impact on postrelease employment experiences. Recidivism was apparently reduced between 3 and 5 percent, but there was little improvement in employment status. Trainees were more likely than controls to be employed full time after three months, probably because of the placement services, but less likely to be employed full time after six months. While trainees earned slightly higher wages, they worked less of the time and tended to earn less overall (Chart 2). Despite the fact that the $1,000 to $1,500 per trainee costs of the MDTA prison projects are about the same as for the overall MDTA training program (and training per se is probably *more* costly since between 30 and 40 percent of MDTA costs are normally for allowances compared with only a fifth of those in prisons), there is no evidence that it has increased employability.

Before concluding that vocational training and supportive services will not work in prisons, it is necessary to break down the aggregate statistics and to consider whether the problems of the 251 projects can be overcome. Experience demonstrated that there are certain individuals who benefit more than others and certain types of training which seem to be more effective. Among trainees the best bet is apparently

CHART 2. THE EMPLOYMENT IMPACTS OF PRISON TRAINING

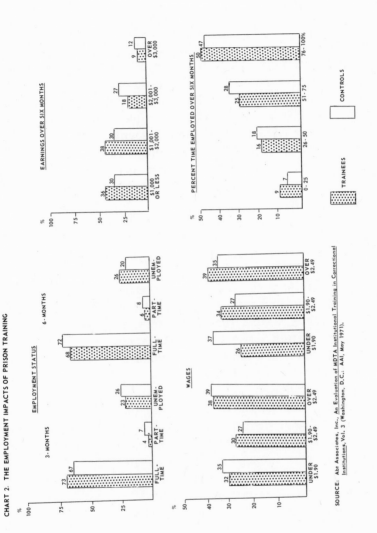

SOURCE: Abt Associates, Inc., _An Evaluation of MDTA Institutional Training in Correctional Institutions_, Vol. 3 (Washington, D.C.: AAI, May 1971).

the better-educated white over-25-year-old, with a previously stable work history. This is hardly surprising, for as under other manpower programs, it is the least disadvantaged who do best. More enlightening are the differences between program offerings. There is evidence that those individuals with extensive counseling and those with more intensive placement services (especially the ones receiving help from both the MDTA staff and the Employment Service) did better in the labor market than those without these benefits. The length or cost of the vocational instruction itself had little straightforward impact on later success, but individuals receiving more intensive basic education tended to do better than those who did not. Trainees also tended to increasingly rate their basic education as the most beneficial component of the program.[46]

In the case of these MDTA projects, deficiencies in the quality and choice of vocational courses may have accounted for their meager impact. Evidence suggested that in many cases the prison staffs conducted "business as usual" with MDTA funds. Rather than initiating innovative courses and fully integrating services into a comprehensive strategy of rehabilitation, they tended to use standard procedures and to merely graft the MDTA program onto ongoing efforts. This is one of the dangers any time an experimental approach is expanded, but especially in the case of prisons, where the intractability of the staffs is a major obstacle. However, it is naive to write off the disappointing results by blaming them on uninspired implementation. In many cases, the prison staffs are made a scapegoat; and in others where they are at fault, their actions may be difficult to change. Prison staffs are part of the prison setting, and they cannot be wished away.

On the other hand, many of the problems in implementing 251 resulted from the inexperience of administrators and the newness of the program. Little central direction was provided by the Department of Labor, and prison staffs sometimes floundered out of ignorance. They might do considerably better on a continuing basis.

Whatever the reasons, the fact remains that the MDTA projects in prisons had very little, if any, impact on employability. Based on available evidence, the conclusion would have to be that vocational training as applied under the "251" program will not be very effective in prisons. Examination of the factors associated with the success of participants revealed that the supportive services rather than the training were associated with individual success. In isolated settings, divorced from labor markets, working with second-rate materials and a highly disadvantaged clientele, vocational training alone seems to have minimal impact. It might be a necessary but not sufficient condition for increasing employability, and its effectiveness might be improved; however, this remains to be demonstrated.

Education for Employment

One of the primary reasons for offenders' problems in the world of work is their lack of education. The typical federal prisoner has completed only nine grades, and less than a fifth of the prisoner population has finished high school.[47] State prisoners have about the same low level of attainment.[48] And as with other disadvantaged groups, measured achievement tends to lag behind these minimal attainment levels. For instance, in one experimental project where each prisoner was given an achievement test, three out of five were at an eighth-grade level or lower, even though four out of five had gone further than this in school; similarly, though nearly three of five reported completing more than nine grades, only a fourth tested out above this level of achievement.[49]

The correlation between education and job success applies to offenders as it does to others. For the offender group as a whole, the low level of attainment places them at the very end of the labor queue. One of the most significant reasons firms will not hire offenders is that employers justifiably believe offenders are undereducated.[50] Those with more schooling do significantly better in the world of work, as the following data on federal releasees indicate (Table 3). This is no proof, but it strongly suggests that increased education will lead to increased employability, at least to the degree that credentials are provided which are acceptable to employers.

PRISON EDUCATION PROGRAMS

Education programs are more frequently offered in prisons than other manpower services, but they still serve only a small proportion of the total population. Among the state prisons with MDTA programs in 1968–69, only 3 percent provided no basic education courses on their own; but in a fifth, less than 5 percent of the inmates participated; and in a third, only between 6 and 20 percent benefited. High school equivalency (GED) courses were less frequent, with a fifth of the prisons having no such program, and only a third serving more than 10 percent of their inmates.[51] Generally speaking, these educational programs are understaffed and under-financed, use archaic methods, and have little impact on participants.

In the past few years, however, some new approaches have been implemented on a small scale. One of these is "pro-

Table 3. Employment Status of Federal Parolees and Mandatory Releasees by Education at Release, June 1964

	9th Grade or Less	10th–11th Grade	12th Grade or More
Employed	79.9	86.0	90.8
Full time	57.0	62.9	79.2
Part time	21.6	22.0	11.0
Unknown	1.3	1.1	.6
Unemployed	20.1	14.0	9.2

SOURCE: Pownall, "Employment Problems," p. 79.

grammed learning," in which each student moves at his own pace through a series of discretely packaged lessons in diverse subjects. The emphasis is on individualized rather than classroom instruction, and frequent use is made of audio and visual equipment. This programmed approach has been applied with some success to help disadvantaged youths in the Job Corps;[52] and when it has been used in prisons, the gains have been comparable. At the Draper Correctional Center in Elmore, Alabama, intensive basic education was provided along with vocational training. In the initial experiment, most inmates received two hours of instruction five days a week for half a year. Teaching machines were used extensively, the pupil-teacher ratio was 12 to 1, and each instructor had a college student aide. As a result of this intensive assistance, participants gained an average of 1.4 grades in their 208 hours of instruction according to standardized achievement tests.[53]

Such statistics undoubtedly exaggerate the gain made by enrollees. Much of what they learned was information they had previously forgotten and would soon forget again. Greater familiarity with testing methods might also account for some of the improvement. And it is also possible that some prisoners recognized the rewards for achievement and purposefully scored low on their initial test. The fact remains, however, that out of almost 400 enrollees, 72 were able to pass the GED.[54] Whether or not this resulted from real educational improvements, they acquired credentials of significant value in the labor market.

Another promising new approach is to provide college-level instruction to better-educated prisoners. It is liberally estimated that there are 30,000 inmates in prisons and jails who could benefit from such opportunities. Project New Gate, which is funded in six different locations by the Office of Economic Opportunity, teaches college courses within correctional facilities, with participants eventually released on parole to continue their education. An early survey found that less than a fifth of participants recidivated within a year of release compared with a much higher percentage of other releasees.[55]

THE POTENTIAL IMPACT

Education programs in prison can have a positive impact on the future work success of participants; and the more intensive the programs, the more favorable the impact will probably be. Chart 3 is based on the experience of trainees in MDTA prison programs. Those who receive basic education are more likely to be employed full time and to work steadily than those who receive other services alone. The more intense the educational program, the more successful the employment experience. Other data suggest that those who pass their GED benefit even more. For instance, in the follow-up of the Draper Project, it was found that men who passed their GED had an average posttraining salary of $350 compared to a $206 pretraining average; non-GED students increased their salary from $240 to only $279.[56]

It is important, however, to recognize the limitations on effective education programs. The physical isolation, the

CHART 3. RELATIONSHIP OF EMPLOYMENT TO HOURS OF BASIC EDUCATION

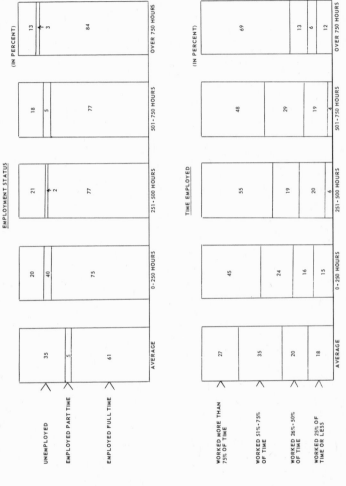

EMPLOYMENT STATUS

(IN PERCENT)

	AVERAGE	0 - 250 HOURS	251 - 500 HOURS	501 - 750 HOURS	OVER 750 HOURS
UNEMPLOYED	35	20	21	18	13
EMPLOYED PART TIME	5	40	2	5	3
EMPLOYED FULL TIME	61	75	77	77	84

TIME EMPLOYED

(IN PERCENT)

	AVERAGE	0 - 250 HOURS	251 - 500 HOURS	501 - 750 HOURS	OVER 750 HOURS
WORKED MORE THAN 75% OF TIME	27	45	55	48	69
WORKED 51% - 75% OF TIME	35	24	19	29	13
WORKED 26% - 50% OF TIME	20	16	20	19	6
WORKED 25% OF TIME OR LESS	18	15	6	4	12

SOURCE: Abt Associates, Evaluation of MDTA Training, Vol. 3.

53

antipathy of personnel, and the negative peer group influences in prison are as much of an obstacle to educational programs as they are to vocational training. More important, however, the short duration of stay of most prisoners means that only marginal gains can be made in education and employment. While specific job skills which permit the offender to perform on a given job can be learned in six months or a year, the contribution of an extra one or two years of achievement has no direct impact on performance, though it may improve it indirectly. Unless education combines with training, or leads to recognized credentials such as the GED, education is not likely to mean much to employers. College education may be worthwhile for some, and others may be able to achieve high school equivalency, but most prisoners are at too low a level to ever attain these credentials. For the minority, education alone may be a worthwhile strategy; but for the majority, it may only be needed to the extent it adds to the effectiveness of other services.

Work in Prison

It is a generally accepted principle that prisoners should work. Costs can be reduced if prisoners handle the maintenance of the institution. They will be reduced even more if prisoner labor or its product can be sold at a profit. The work experience itself may have some rehabilitative impact, and skills picked up on the job may be carried over to private life.

Disagreement comes over the purposes and kinds of work which should be done. Laws have been passed at the state and federal level to restrict the use of prison labor, partially to protect against exploitation and partially to eliminate competition. For the most part, the interstate transportation of convict-made goods is now prohibited; and state prisons produce largely for state use, for example, making automobile licenses, renovating furniture, and recapping tires. Executive order restricts the federal government from buying the products of these state prisons. Most federal institutions have their own industries operated by a nonprofit corporation, Federal Prison Industries, Inc., whose products are usually sold at competitive prices to the federal government.

JOBS BEHIND BARS

It is difficult to get an accurate census of prison industries. Federal Prison Industries, Inc., employed an average of 4,800, or roughly a fourth, of all federal prisoners in fiscal 1970, with a $6.3 million profit on sales of $52.4 million to federal agencies.[57] But there are no data on the state prison industries or on the maintenance work assignments in either state or federal prisons. Nevertheless, some idea can be gained from piecing together available information. An extensive survey of federal releasees in 1964 found that less than a third had worked in industries while the rest worked in maintenance. Most of the jobs were unskilled or semiskilled (Table 4).

In the 30 state institutions with MDTA programs in 1968–69, it was found that 7 had no formal industrial program, 19 had highly production-oriented programs, and 4 had rehabilitation-oriented efforts. Among the inmates who worked in industries, 4 percent worked less than 20 hours per

Table 4. Prison Work Assignment of Federal Parolees, 1964

Work Assignment	Percent of Parolees with Particular Work Assignment
None or full-time school	1.2
Maintenance, unskilled	33.5
Maintenance, semi-skilled	15.9
Maintenance, skilled	8.9
Industries	28.9
Typing or other clerical	11.5

SOURCE: Pownall, "Employment Problems," p. 99.

week; 80 percent, between 20 and 40; and 16 percent, over 40. The assessment of work experience in these institutions is probably applicable to all state prisons.

In most projects, inmates rarely had a choice regarding particular work assignments. Work was either unavailable to all inmates. . .or was an institutional requirement which often resulted in "make-work" programs. Wages, often set by state law, varied from $.10 per day to $1.00 per day . . . . The degrading and irrelevant nature of most of these activities, in terms of improving the inmates' post-release employment prospects, stands in sharp contrast to most of the 251 (MDTA) training course activity.[58]

THE IMPACT OF WORK EXPERIENCE

The hope that prisoners will be rehabilitated by their work experience or by the acquisition of on-the-job skills is not borne out by the evidence. For instance, postrelease survey data indicate that participants in federal prison industries are more likely to be unemployed upon release than those involved in unskilled maintenance (Table 5). While persons with no work assignments are likely to do worse afterwards than those who worked, the reason is clearly that the mentally and physically handicapped and the behavioral problems are usually the ones excepted from assignment.

Table 5. Employment Experience of Federal Releasees by Prison Assignment

	Percent of Total	Percent with This Assignment	Employment Status			
			Employed	Full Time	Part Time	Unemployed
None, or full-time school	1.2	100.0	72.7	54.5	18.2	27.3
Maintenance, unskilled labor	33.5	100.0	82.9	60.3	22.7	17.1
Industries	28.9	100.0	81.0	62.6	18.4	19.0
Typing or other clerical	11.5	100.0	81.6	68.0	13.6	18.4
Maintenance, semi-skilled	15.9	100.0	86.6	64.6	22.0	13.4
Maintenance, skilled	8.9	100.0	89.9	69.9	20.0	10.1
Total	–	100.0	83.3	63.3	20.0	16.7

SOURCE: Pownall, "Employment Problems," p. 99.

Another indication of limited success is that only 15 percent of releasees found a related first job, and only 20 percent eventually moved into work which was training- or experience-related.

WASTED MANPOWER

The most basic manpower problem in the prisons is that they do not effectively utilize their human resources. With limited markets for their goods, they can employ only a minority of inmates in prison industries. The rest are applied to maintenance tasks with little concern for efficiency or output. When labor is a relatively free good, it is almost always misused.

Prison industries, in particular, have a number of short-comings. Operating with out-of-date equipment and producing a limited range of specialized products, they teach few skills that can be carried over into the outside world. As examples of the types of jobs which are provided and of their values, a study of three federal prisons found that in the furniture refurbishing operations of one, only five of the fifty-six jobs were considered to have marketable value; in another, valuable reupholstering skills could be learned, but only a small number of "senior" inmates were given these jobs; while in the third prison, the tire retreading operations taught up-to-date skills and were highly profitable.[59]

A major problem is that the skills and abilities of inmates are rarely used to their fullest extent. Job assignments are often made on the basis of seniority, docility, length of sentence, or other criteria which may bear little relation to productivity. Work assignments in prisons have only a rough correlation with occupation before confinement, except in the cases of those with clerical and operative experience (Table 6).

A final problem of prison industries is the lack of effective incentives for productivity. There are a number of incentives

Table 6. Prison Work Assignment by Occupation before Last Confinement

(in percent)

	Total	Never Employed	Manager	Clerical, Sales	Skilled	Operative	Service	Unskilled
Industries	29	12	25	16	29	42	36	32
Clerical	16	13	25	56	—	8	29	5
Maintenance, skilled	14	16	25	12	21	10	21	11
Maintenance, semi-skilled	18	20	25	12	21	16	7	24
Maintenance, unskilled	23	39	—	4	29	24	7	28

SOURCE: Pownall, "Employment Problems," p. 101.
NOTE: Excludes those in school or not assigned.

which could be used in the prison setting that are unavailable on the outside: activity assignments including work release, recognition, "good time" towards parole, quarters assignments and freedoms. Money is also especially effective since there is usually no alternative way for the prisoner to meet present and future needs. Unfortunately, these incentives are rarely utilized to motivate increased production in prison industries. Wages are often paid to all workers at the same hourly rate; supervisory positions are earned through good behavior rather than job performance; work release is based on parole dates and job availability rather than effectiveness in work.

ECONOMIC DEVELOPMENT OF PRISONS

One possible way to overcome these problems is to attract competitive private businesses to the prisons, which will have their choice of inmates with minimal restrictions, will pay market wages based on productivity (some proportion of which can be paid to the prison for room and board), and will produce goods for sale in the outside market. This is, in fact, what is being tried by The Urban Coalition, which is searching for some small branch factories that are willing to locate at the Lorton Reformatory outside Washington, D.C.

This approach certainly deserves some experimental effort. To make it succeed, state and federal laws may need to be amended concerning the sale of prison-made goods. In particular, Executive Order 325, which forbids the use of prisoners in the performance of federal contracts and restricts the purchase of state and prison goods by the federal government or its contractors, would have to be modified.

Nevertheless, the obvious drawbacks to this approach should be recognized at the outset. Attracting businesses to any isolated location is difficult, and to find those which are willing to work with the hard-core disadvantaged within the prison setting is not likely to be easy. There are limits to how much prison officials will agree to relax their rules, and outside industries will create many detention problems. But most of all, unions and other businesses are likely to complain about the unfair competition from prison industries if they become effective competitors. On an ad hoc, limited basis, industries might be introduced—for instance, blood donor facilities servicing the inmate population—but large-scale economic development efforts would draw extensive criticism from vested interests. Nevertheless, ad hoc efforts may be effective in attracting competitive businesses to prison.

Work Release

Perhaps the best way of giving prisoners valuable work experience is to release them for jobs in the public and private sector. Working full time during the day and returning to the prison at night, the prisoner will be under some discipline and control without being removed completely from the economic mainstream. Out of the prisoner's earnings, maintenance costs can be repaid, he can be given an allowance, and his family can be supported or else he can save a nest egg to cushion his release. Rather than wasting his prison time in unproductive work, he can be making a positive contribution to society.

Recognizing these potential benefits, the Prison Rehabilitation Act of 1965 authorized work release for federal prisoners; and a number of state laws have been changed so that thirty states and the District of Columbia now permit work release. Despite this mandate, only a small minority of those nearing probation are allowed to seek jobs outside. Isolated prison locations and transportation difficulties often rule out this approach. And in many cases, the custodial staff is reluctant to give any special help to those they consider security risks. As a result, less than a tenth of all federal prisoners participated in work release programs in fiscal 1970. At the state level, 14 of the 25 projects with MDTA programs in 1968–69 had no work release program, 8 had a minimum program serving 10 percent or less of the total population, and only 3 (which contained only 7 percent of the sample population) had between 11 and 20 percent of their inmates on work release. The following assessment of work release in these prisons could probably be applied to most state institutions.

In general, work release programs—if offered at all—were available only to inmates with minimum security status who were within the last few months of their sentence and who were likely to receive parole board approval. . . . Prison administrators considered only productive workers with "clean records" as eligible for employment in the community. Most work release programs established these criteria under administrative rather than legislative authority. Thus eligibility criteria restricted the scope and usefulness of work release as an auxiliary program service.[60]

At the local level, there is apparently even less effective use of work release. Yet this is perhaps where it could have the greatest impact. The majority of prisoners are either awaiting trial or serving short terms; and once in jail, they lose their jobs even though their offense and sentence may be minor. Since most local jails are in close proximity to jobs, many prisoners could keep working while they were serving time. This would alleviate transitional employment problems and could substantially reduce the costs of jail.

61

A VIABLE ALTERNATIVE

The Federal Bureau of Prisons has carried out a follow-up study of prisoners who were in the work release program in fiscal 1967. Overall, their recidivism seems to be lower than the prison norm. Among adults, 77 percent succeed, that is, they are not recommitted for a felony offense or a parole or misdemeanor violation. This percentage might be compared with the dated figures of a 1956 study of adult releasees which showed a success rate of only 67 percent. It must be remembered, however, that prisoners with the cleanest records and least chances of recidivism were the ones selected for work release. Thus, there was no significant difference in the later recidivism of those who successfully completed work release and those who either escaped while on release or were removed because of community or institutional infractions; this suggests that work release itself might have had little to do with any reduced recidivism.[61]

Whatever its impact on the future criminal behavior of the individual, work release must also be judged relative to its immediate alternatives—prison and probation. The earnings of work releasees must be weighed against the costs related to individualized attention and the recapture of escaped releasees. The prison personnel's concern with security has some basis. Of the 1,536 federal work releasees in fiscal 1967, 190 were removed from the program for offenses of one sort or another and 124 escaped. Finding jobs and making transportation arrangements for those on work release involve some costs, as do the crimes the prisoners commit while on release and the efforts which must be exerted to recapture escapees. Despite these problems, there can be little doubt that when jobs are available, and the more reliable prisoners are chosen to participate, work release can be much more economic than full-time prison simply because the individual, rather than society, foots the bill. In the first fourteen months of the federal work release program, some two thousand inmates paid state and federal taxes amounting to $303,000, sent $327,000 home for families, saved $700,000, spent $572,000 in the local communities, and paid the prison system $203,000 for upkeep. This more than $2 million in inmate earnings was for the most part a net addition to the economy and the individuals.[62]

Nevertheless, while work release may be preferable to prison, there is little reason to assume that it is preferable to early parole. Though it permits some continued control over the individual, and eases his transition back into the community, it also may involve lengthy transportation or else may require the prisoner to work in a job near the institution which is far less productive than one he could acquire elsewhere. Research is needed to test the comparative effectiveness of work release and earlier parole (which could perhaps be made conditional on the maintenance of employment).

MANPOWER SERVICES FOR WORK RELEASEES

If work release is to be expanded, manpower services must play a more significant role. The local employment service must develop jobs and provide placement and counseling for early releasees. Links must be established with the prison, coordinating work release with vocational training and using work release as a stimulus for better performance in this training. This, in turn, would mean working with those individuals who are most likely to benefit from such services rather than those with the "cleanest records" or those who are nearest to their parole date. Manpower considerations should figure prominently in these decisions. In this context, it is important to note some of the rather surprising findings of the previously mentioned follow-up study of federal work releasees conducted by the Federal Bureau of Prisons.

First, drug offenders tended to be more successful than other former prisoners, with a success rate of 79 percent compared with the 77 percent rate overall, though most of the difference is accounted for by the especially high success rate of marijuana offenders.[63]

Second, youthful offenders who participate tend to do much worse than older ones, though participation somewhat delays their usual patterns of recidivism.

And third, the personal characteristics that affect success, such as education, age at first offense, number of prior offenses, type of crime, and race, do not serve as very good predictors (though the opposite has been found in another study of work releasees[64]). This suggests the need for more careful identification of prisoners' employability characteristics and their relation to success during and after work release.

Quite obviously, however, the success of any work release program depends on the availability of jobs. If prisons are located in areas where there are labor shortages, prisoners trained or skilled in shortage occupations will be easy to place. But when there are slack labor markets, and the placement agencies must chose between helping either disadvantaged nonoffenders (and ex-offenders already returned to the community) or prisoners, who are not considered members of the community, work release will be difficult to implement.

Intensive Postrelease Services

Postrelease manpower and supportive services may be provided as a continuation of in-prison programs or used as an alternative strategy for assisting the prison population. These services may be delivered through the parole system and other community agencies or concentrated in special institutions, such as half-way houses.

There are a number of conceptual attractions to immediate postrelease services. First, they can ease the transition from prison life to community life. Specific problems can be met as they arise, and the participant can be kept occupied during the critical period of adjustment. Second, postrelease services can fully utilize community facilities, which may prove more effective than trying to duplicate these facilities in the prison setting. And third, intensive services permit closer tabs on the individual to catch him whenever he begins to wander. These potential benefits would appear to be especially important in dealing with young, first and second offenders, since they have the greatest employment and transition problems and the highest rates of recidivism. Older releasees with greater opportunities to work and longer work experience are probably more concerned with jobs than services; but they, too, might benefit.

MEAGER HELP

For the most part, parolees are left on their own to sink or swim. Parole staffs are clearly overburdened, and they can do little outside of checking against violations. For instance, the National Council on Crime and Delinquency found that in 1965 there were 63,000 adult prisoners paroled from state prisons and 102,000 already on parole; at the same time, there were only 1,800 parole officers or roughly one for every sixty parolees (compared with a parolee standard of thirty-five now considered optimal). Some states, such as New York, have parole personnel specifically assigned to help with employment problems; but the number of personnel is totally inadequate to the task, and parolees normally receive little assistance in finding or holding jobs.[65]

Over the last decade, however, there has been a dramatic proliferation of community facilities to supplement parole services. The 1969 Directory of Half-Way Houses identified 97 community institutions serving parolees; all but 13 of the institutions had been established in the sixties and have drawn a great deal of attention, though the aggregate impact is limited. Total capacity for institutions serving parolees, as well as alcoholics, addicts, runaways, vagrants, probationers, and the mentally deficient, was only around 3,000, with almost half of this number located in California. Most half-way houses serve only a handful of offenders. And usually, very few services are provided outside of room and board and some superficial counseling.[66]

These community facilities are sometimes the focus of intensive controversy. For instance, in Washington, D.C. several half-way houses were closed after highly publicized crimes by residents. It is difficult to interpret exactly what the risks are in this type of treatment or the probabilities of success. In the District's program, 1,073 adults resided in the half-way houses at some time in fiscal 1971; most but not all were parolees. Two-fifths of the total terminated "unacceptably," with 8 percent committing new crimes, 18 percent absconding, and the remainder returning to prison for violation of house rules. Whether this is a good or bad record is difficult to judge; but members of the community were alarmed by the proximity of potential criminals, and their fears had some justification.[67]

PROJECT DEVELOP

Perhaps the most careful effort to measure the impact of postrelease manpower services was in Project Develop, operated under a grant from the Department of Labor to the New York State Division of Parole. Running between 1966 and 1968, Project Develop provided vocational guidance, work orientation, counseling, education, training, support, placement, and follow-up assistance to young (17- to 23-year-old), undereducated and underemployed parolees with above-average intelligence. There were 115 program completers, of which seventy-one were referred to trade schools, MDTA, union, or antipoverty organization training. The total costs were roughly $2,400 per completer, counting the MDTA costs but not those of the other training programs.

Unfortunately, the chief interest of the parole personnel was to reduce recidivism rather than to increase employability. A control group was carefully selected, but it was only used to assess the program's impact on criminal behavior. The results, however, are instructive. Among the Project Develop completers, 15 percent violated parole or were rearrested for a new crime within the two- to ten-month period involved, compared with 23 percent of the controls. Only 6 percent of the experimental group were sent back to jail, compared with 12 percent of the controls. Although these differences are not statistically significant, they suggest that the manpower services had a favorable impact on recidivism.

A closer look, however, raises doubts about this success. The control group was chosen to match the completer group rather than the total number enrolled in Project Develop. Of the 209 enrollees, 15 dropped out in good standing, 3 absconded from supervision, and 35 others were arrested and/or returned to jail. If the controls had been compared to all these participants, they would have done *better* on the average than those receiving services.

In assessing the impact of any postrelease services, it is also necessary to take a long-run view. While there may be an immediate impact on employment and recidivism, the results may fade as participants move out from under supervision. This, as noted earlier, was to some extent the case in Project Crossroads; and it is likely that much the same thing happens with parolees. Though postponement of recidivism is not an inappropriate goal, it may indicate that the services have had less effect than the supervision and use of parolees' time. The Project Develop follow-up did not have a long enough time span to test this possibility.[68]

THE IMPLICATIONS

When offenders are released from prison, there is no doubt that they have transition problems; but there is no proof that intensive manpower services help to alleviate them. Older releasees are usually disinterested in further discipline and delay of gratification. Younger releasees may need other types of assistance. However, a substantial minority may benefit. The key is to establish criteria to identify those who are most likely to gain from manpower services and to restrict services to them.

To date, the limited evidence does not disprove the effectiveness of this approach. Further experimentation is needed, for instance, in utilizing Job Corps centers to train some releasees. An effort should be made to link prison training, work release, parole, and probation to a half-way house and then to total release, in a continuum as was done to some extent in Project First Chance in South Carolina and Project Fresh Start in Detroit.

Income Maintenance during Postrelease Adjustment

The unemployment insurance and welfare systems provide relief during periods of layoff for most workers to make up for lost income and to cushion the transition back into the labor market. The assumption is that many workers lack the personal resources to weather the income loss without severe hardship and that their search for jobs will be more rational if they are less desperate.

Offenders released from prisons and jails have a difficult transition back into the labor market. They have very limited resources as a rule, usually depending on the pittance given them upon release. With all their difficulties, success in the world of work demands a careful rather than desperate search for jobs. Yet ex-prisoners are usually ineligible for unemployment insurance benefits and in most localities cannot receive welfare.

The conceptual arguments for income maintenance during postrelease adjustment are compelling. First, ex-convicts face severe adjustment problems. Though some have jobs arranged before they leave prison, many must search for and find a job immediately if they are to survive. A study of federal releasees found that 54 percent had no job arranged, and 9 percent had a job but did not report; the majority of the remainder were those on parole for whom employment was usually a condition of release, whether or not their job suited their best interests.

Second, prisoners rarely have any resources to fall back on during the transition. Though conditions have undoubtedly improved, a study[69] in 1960 found that most prisons supply $40 or less "gate money" for releasees, with many providing nothing. Releasees have little cushion if they cannot find jobs immediately. Even if they can find employment, it is difficult to accumulate reserves for an emergency with the low wages most of them earn. For instance, data on federal releasees revealed that after three months more than half the releasees remaining free had not even accumulated $50 (Table 7). Any unusual circumstance would quickly exhaust these reserves and would make crime a temptation.

Table 7. Resources of Federal Releasees, 1965

| | Percentage Distribution | | | |
	Cash at Release	Cash at End of First Month[a]	Cash at End of Second Month[a]	Cash at End of Third Month[a]
Less than $50	45	58	52	32
50–99	43	10	13	16
100–199	8	7	11	3
200 or more	4	18	21	26
No information	–	7	3	3

SOURCE: Pownall, "Employment Problems," pp. 182, 184, and 199.

[a]Only those who remain in the community without rearrest or reincarceration.

Third, with no other options, ex-convicts are more likely than others to turn to the skill they know best—crime. Nine out of ten prisoners are in prison for stealing or trying to steal someone else's property. Feeling that their criminal skills have improved with "institutional training," they may be strongly tempted to put them to the test if they are discouraged by failures in the world of work. The majority of backsliders are rearrested within the first three to six months after release,[70] which is the most difficult period of adjustment. If income were provided during this time, however, ex-prisoners might be able to make the transition and move into stable patterns of work.

EXPERIENCE WITH INCOME SUPPLEMENTS

The logic of these arguments has not evaded policymakers. In a number of experimental and demonstration projects, income payments have been used as a supplement to other services. In the Rikers Island Project, for instance, "loans" (only 3 percent of which were repaid) were made to trainees, not exceeding $200 apiece but averaging only $50 for completers.[71] Whether these monies contributed to the "success" of participants cannot be determined. The Draper Project in Elmore, Alabama, provided lump-sum grants averaging around $90 for trainees to relocate from the rural prison. Apparently, the grants had little impact since the releasees tended to "blow" their income on nonessentials. The conclusion of the Draper Project was that transitional monies were still needed, but stricter controls had to be exercised over their use.[72]

The most extensive experiment with money payments was under a number of vocational rehabilitation projects in 1967-69. Roughly 250 offenders received an average of approximately $1,000, with some receiving almost twice this amount. There was no noticeable improvement in the employability or recidivism of participants, making it difficult to support the claim that income maintenance is worthwhile. This, nonetheless, is the assertion of the rehabilitation staff.

Often, the provision of maintenance did no good. The receipt of basic subsistence, some pocket cash, and the supportive counseling that usually accompanied these expenditures could still leave a need that demanded the return to criminal activity. Sometimes clients simply could not make the transition from the structured environment of prison to the competitive free world, from the excitement of crime to the less sanguinary pleasures of a "square-jober" life, no matter, how much money was available to them.

Yet despite these considerations, the. . . provision of maintenance would still be passionately defended by most. . . counselors. They know that $40 gate money upon release from prison, or whatever it may be, will not keep a man, newly reintroduced to the pleasures of the free world, until receipt of first pay.[73]

THE NEED FOR EXPERIMENTATION

It might be argued that offenders have "paid their debt to society" and deserve help like other disadvantaged persons to overcome the transitional employment difficulties. Nevertheless, it is unlikely that society will allocate a scarce resource to this aspect of corrections unless there are demonstrated results in terms of quantitative or qualitative improvements in employment and reductions in recidivism. As yet, the conceptual benefits of income maintenance during post-release have not been demonstrated.

The Labor Department is now funding a project in Baltimore to test the individual and combined effects of income maintenance and employment assistance. Some prisoners will receive financial aid and manpower services, other prisoners will receive only one or the other, and a control group will receive neither. The results of this study should suggest whether larger scale implementation is needed, and whether changes should eventually be made in unemployment insurance regulations and prison "gate money" provisions.[74]

Job Development and Placement Services

The payoff of any manpower service is placement in a job. As the high unemployment rate of offenders indicates, the follow-through to the placement stage is often lacking, and on their own, many offenders cannot get jobs. When placements are made, they usually entail low-paying and unattractive jobs offering little inducement to the offender to readjust to the world of work.

There is copious documentation for this shortcoming. Among releasees from federal prisons, more than half do not have prearranged jobs. Four out of five of those prearranged were found through friends, family, or former employers, without any help from public agencies. Only 5 to 10 percent of ex-prisoners get help from the Employment Service in finding their first job, and almost none turn to it later in their careers. Less than a fourth of those who find jobs apply the work experience or training acquired in prison.[75] The best placement, job development, and follow-up services in the world will not help many prisoners, especially those who remain unskilled and poorly educated. And these services will have little impact when aggregate unemployment is high and jobs are scarce. Nevertheless, improved job development and placement can be worthwhile under normal conditions and in combination with other efforts.

MDTA EXPERIENCE

The potential effectiveness of placement services is suggested by the experience of participants in prison MDTA projects. According to the guidelines for the program, the U.S. Employment and Training Service was to have responsibility for providing a continuum of prerelease to postrelease services—counseling prisoners as to work alternatives, determining their abilities and preferences, finding meaningful jobs appropriate to their needs, making the actual placements, and providing follow-up services for employers and employees to help in their mutual adjustment.

In general, the response of the local employment services to this mandate was not very impressive. Only a third of trainees were helped by active ES effort and 7 percent by a combination of ES and MDTA staff efforts. Ten percent received no placement services, 19 percent were limited to the standard ES referral assistance, and the rest were helped by the MDTA staff or some other agency. A careful analysis of the overall experience reached the following rather negative assessment.

The study did expect to find some projects in which job developers work initially with job candidates and then move out to employers to tailor jobs for these candidates. Moreover, the study anticipated that for most projects there would be "an attempt to develop a system of supportive services for new workers and the employers to facilitate jobs for the hard-to-employ;" and, that at least to a limited extent, projects would have "an organization of diverse skills and expertise. . . to create new jobs by eliminating traditional barriers to employment." Such activities were rarely found in practice.[76]

Before considering the reasons for these shortcomings, it is instructive to look at the differential impact when more intensive services were provided. When jobs were "developed," participants tended to have better employment experience, though recidivism was apparently not reduced: 78 percent of those in developed jobs worked full time, compared with 73 percent of those in other jobs; 53 percent had worked three-fourths of the time since release, compared with only 40 percent of the others; 55 percent were in training-related jobs, compared with 45 percent of those whose jobs were not developed. There is also evidence that the different delivery systems for development and placement services vary in effectiveness. In the minority of cases when the Employment Service took an active role, the results were most effective (Chart 4). When trainees received no help, results were least effective. Standard ES procedures proved to be better than nothing, but not nearly as good as intensive efforts.

Given the apparent effectiveness of intensive placement and job development services for *trained* prisoners, it is vital to determine why these services were not more widely implemented. One reason was inherent in the "pilot" nature of the program; given its limited horizons, there was little incentive to allocate already scarce staff time to these activities and too little time to develop the necessary contacts with employers. A second reason was the prison setting. Most prisons are geographically isolated, ruling out employer contacts and

CHART 4. RELATION OF EMPLOYMENT STATUS TO PLACEMENT STRATEGY

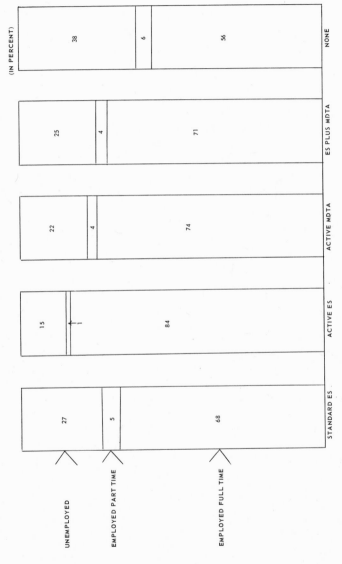

SOURCE: Abt Associates, Evaluation of MDTA Training, Vol. 3.

restricting job interviews, which are also limited by often inflexible regulations. A single prison may serve a geographical area of hundreds of square miles, and releasees may locate in any of a number of labor markets. It is difficult to coordinate placement and job development services in all possible locations.

Another problem is that to obtain parole prisoners often have to show proof of employment. More than anything else, they want to get out; and most are unwilling to wait for the ideal job, taking what they can get without effort. Unless the Employment Service moves in effectively prior to the parole date, prisoners will use other means to find jobs. But since parole is uncertain, it is difficult to arrange jobs before the fact; employers who agree to hire a prisoner who is not subsequently released are unlikely to do so again.

Perhaps the major obstacle, however, is the unwillingness of the ES staff to take on new functions. Already overloaded in serving a basically disadvantaged clientele, they are rarely interested in assuming even more difficult responsibilities. The Employment Service as a whole is not distinguished by its adaptability to innovative ideas; and in this case, there are few incentives inducing them to change their ways. For instance, in the Draper Project in Elmore, Alabama, placements were initially handled by the project staff; later this responsibility was shifted to the Alabama State Employment Service. Training-related placements fell off noticeably, and an investigation to discover the cause found that the ES offices outside of Elmore were simply unwilling to offer offenders any more than the standard assistance.[77]

THE MODEL EX-OFFENDER PROGRAM

To find out whether the Employment Service can effectively assist offenders, the Labor Department is funding a pilot effort in five states to improve the kind, quality, and relevance of manpower services for persons with arrest records. The five states have been allocated $3.6 million to hire personnel who, working in the institutions as well as in the community, will make special efforts to counsel offenders, coordinate local services, and develop jobs for and place parolees. Additional money is provided to cover training costs of ex-offenders.

As yet, there is no evidence on the impact of these services. If one judges from the steps taken to implement the program to date, it is unlikely services will make more than a marginal contribution, especially in the present economic climate.

For one thing, little energy has been directed to advertising the program or soliciting support from the community. The Employment Service is extremely sensitive to public sentiment against "mollycoddling" prisoners; and rather than trying to change this sentiment, local offices have contented themselves with working surreptitiously.

Most of the local ES offices have apparently viewed the offender program as an extension of their present duties. Another staff person is found to do the same thing in the same way for a different clientele. This may be successful to some degree, as the experience of prison MDTA participants receiving standard services indicates; but more intensive efforts may be needed. This will be especially true when prisoners who have *not* received MDTA or other training are being helped.

The Employment Service does not have the leverage to coordinate the activities of other public and private agencies. The ex-prisoner may need any of a wide variety of services if he is to adjust successfully to work, but there is no way the ES can force other groups to add offenders to the already overburdened caseloads.

Finally, the ES is not likely to reach out to many ex-prisoners. Few paraprofessionals or others having sensitivity to and experience with offenders are being hired by the ES. As a rule, prisoners would rather use other means of finding a job. A survey of releasees found that 75 percent had never used the Employment Service, because they had a bad impression of it, lacked knowledge, or could find employment on their own. Almost all expressed dissatisfaction with its red tape and depersonalized service. And a third indicated that they would rather take a chance on hiding their criminal record from employers.[78] It is revealing that almost all of the interviewed prisoners were against any further training programs outside of the job. They were more concerned with money and work rather than longer range goals.

Whether the Model Ex-Offender Program will overcome these difficulties remains to be seen. If it does not succeed, it may only mean that the ES is not the best delivery system for placement and job development services, not that these services are unimportant.

SERVING OTHER OFFENDERS

Parolees and recently released prisoners are a minority of the offender population, and perhaps the most difficult segment to work with. It is likely that placement and job development assistance could have a greater impact on probationers and those awaiting trial. The Employment Service might be an effective means of providing these services, as well as an entry point into the manpower system. The courts could use their authority to refer offenders with obvious employment problems to the local ES.

This approach is certainly worth testing. The Model Ex-Offender Program is serving only ex-prisoners. Similar experiments need to be instituted which provide services to probationers and pretrial arrestees. Though it is difficult to foresee the ES being any more innovative and successful in this area than in other efforts to help the hard-core disadvantaged, there are few practical alternatives.

The Systems Approach

There are obviously a wide range of services and strategies which could reasonably be expected to help the offender overcome his employment problems. Rarely, if ever, can these be weighed separately and compared with alternatives. For instance, pretrial counseling, training, and placement do not deal with the same clientele or have to cope with the same problems as postrelease efforts; it is misleading but all too easy to conclude that either the pretrial or the postrelease programs are more effective in helping offenders when in fact the two programs are oriented toward two different populations. Only if the problem is reduced to cost-benefit terms with a determination of the marginal increase in employment and decrease in crime for each dollar spent, and only if policymakers are willing to make their decisions on these rather abstract grounds, can a straightforward choice be made. Needless to say, there is little likelihood that this will ever occur.

The problem of complementarities is even more perplexing. The effectiveness of any single service may depend on the availability of others; counseling and placement may have little impact without training or institutional change, and vice versa. Almost all projects combine a variety of services, and it is difficult to isolate the contribution of any one. In those projects which emphasize a single approach, shortcomings are usually blamed on the dearth of needed outside services.

THE MYTH OF SYSTEMATIC SOLUTIONS

The easy claim is that a "systems approach" is the key, where assistance will be provided on a one-stop but comprehensive basis, tailored to individual need. If an offender requires only handholding, as some undoubtedly do, he should not be slotted into a training program. If he is educated but lacks a saleable skill, he should receive vocational instruction. If he is trained but is unable to get a job because of bonding difficulties, he should be provided a bond. This is self-evident.

What is not self-evident is the means of determining the needs of each individual and the best way of providing him services. Clearly, some poorly educated trainees will fail in any vocational program; but on the other hand, there are some skills which can be taught to those with very limited educations. Counseling may be needed by an individual, or it may prove worthless, merely delaying him from attaining other more vital services, perhaps even undermining his future by nurturing false expectations. Though some progress has been made towards the classification of offenders, the state of the art is still too limited to match up services with individual needs except in the crudest fashion. Even if both services and needs can be identified, they cannot necessarily be provided in every case. The sole purpose of the court and corrections system is not to rehabilitate; and whatever is done, there are constraints on what can be offered. The delivery agency must choose among existing options and work within the existing correctional regulations.

THE EXPERIENCE WITH VOCATIONAL
REHABILITATION

The difficulties are well illustrated by the experience with offenders under the Vocational Rehabilitation Program (VR) Traditionally, this program has dealt with the mentally and physically handicapped, providing counseling and diagnostic services, while purchasing other needed assistance from hospitals and assorted agencies. Given the success of its individualized, case-by-case approach, legislative changes in 1965 and 1968 extended its mandate to include the "socio-economically disadvantaged," as well as the mentally and physically handicapped.

Beginning in early 1966, projects were started in eleven cities providing VR services to offenders. Field personnel were instructed to use innovative approaches and were given a blank check in serving probationers, prisoners, and parolees. Concentrating on a typically disadvantaged offender clientele, the Vocational Rehabilitation projects provided maintenance, training, tools, hospitalization, counseling, and hospital care according to the individual needs of its 510 participants (Chart 5). The following table gives the average cost and percentage receiving these services (Table 8).

To measure the impact of these efforts, a control group of 602 was selected which matched up closely with those receiv-

Table 8. Services Offered under the Vocational Rehabilitation Projects for Offenders

Service	Average Cost Per Recipient	Average Percent Received
VR Diagnostic	87	100
Counseling[a]	380	100
Contract Diagnostic	90	50
Surgery and Treatment	230	33
Prosthesis	100	14
Hospitalization	390	7
Training	670	50
Maintenance	1,030	62

SOURCE: E. M. Oliver et al., *A Future for Correctional Rehabilitation?* (Olympia, Wash.: Division of Vocational Rehabilitation, Coordinating Service for Occupational Education, 1969).

[a]An average of 18.9 hours were received, valued at $20 per hour.

CHART 5. CHARACTERISTICS OF OFFENDERS IN VOCATIONAL REHABILITATION PROJECTS

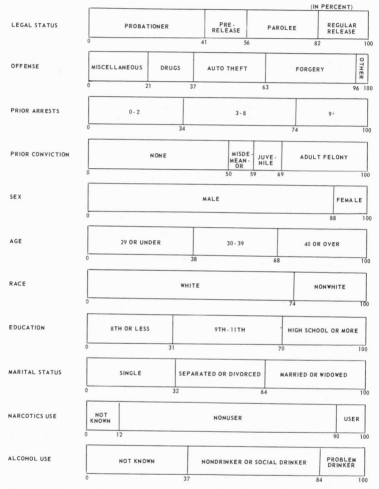

(IN PERCENT)

LEGAL STATUS — PROBATIONER | PRE-RELEASE | PAROLEE | REGULAR RELEASE
0 ... 41 ... 56 ... 82 ... 100

OFFENSE — MISCELLANEOUS | DRUGS | AUTO THEFT | FORGERY | OTHER
0 ... 21 ... 37 ... 63 ... 96 ... 100

PRIOR ARRESTS — 0-2 | 3-8 | 9+
0 ... 34 ... 74 ... 100

PRIOR CONVICTION — NONE | MISDEMEANOR | JUVENILE | ADULT FELONY
0 ... 50 ... 59 ... 69 ... 100

SEX — MALE | FEMALE
0 ... 88 ... 100

AGE — 29 OR UNDER | 30-39 | 40 OR OVER
0 ... 38 ... 68 ... 100

RACE — WHITE | NONWHITE
0 ... 74 ... 100

EDUCATION — 8TH OR LESS | 9TH-11TH | HIGH SCHOOL OR MORE
0 ... 31 ... 70 ... 100

MARITAL STATUS — SINGLE | SEPARATED OR DIVORCED | MARRIED OR WIDOWED
0 ... 32 ... 64 ... 100

NARCOTICS USE — NOT KNOWN | NONUSER | USER
0 ... 12 ... 90 ... 100

ALCOHOL USE — NOT KNOWN | NONDRINKER OR SOCIAL DRINKER | PROBLEM DRINKER
0 ... 37 ... 84 ... 100

SOURCE: E.M. Oliver et al., A Future for Correctional Rehabilitation? (Olympia, Wash.: Division of Vocational Rehabilitation, Coordinating Service for Occupational Education, 1969).

82

ing VR services. Follow-up and comparison of the two groups, subsequent experience revealed, if anything, the *negative* impact of the program. Participants receiving intensive services were slightly *more* likely to be rearrested, convicted, and returned to jail than controls. Controls on the average were employed 83 percent of the time they were in the community, compared with 78 percent of the time for those receiving intensive services. After two years, intensives were more likely to be employed as white-collar workers, but less likely to work in the higher paying machine trades.[79]

These results, like others, do not prove that Vocational Rehabilitation services are of no use to the offender population. There are many drawbacks to the experiment, as its administrators will quickly admit. Nevertheless, it should be clear that the "systems approach" with individualized service is no panacea and has yet to prove its effectiveness in helping offenders.

BEYOND REACH?

These negative results of the Vocational Rehabilitation experiment, weighed in light of the very limited success of other services and combinations of services, must raise doubts about our present capacity to increase the employability of offenders. The meager impact may be due to the inadequacies of the assistance or the way it is delivered. It may also result from the inherent inability of the offender to benefit from any help, since he may no longer be salvagable by the time he becomes an offender. Or alternatively, the modest results may be proof that the fault lies outside the individual. In this case, the solution would not be individual rehabilitation but institutional change: the reform of prisons and jails, the creation of new types of correctional institutions, the elimination of unwarranted employer prejudice against offenders and of artificial barriers to their employment, and the opening of new jobs in the public sector.

However, while these strategies for institutional change need to be carefully examined in turn, the fact remains that the offender population is, on the average, extremely disadvantaged. If nothing can be done to improve offenders' education, work habits, job skills, and general acceptability to employers, employment problems are likely to remain severe no matter what changes are made elsewhere.

Removing Barriers to Employment

The employment problems of offenders result not only from their personal deficiencies and transitional difficulties but also from their restricted opportunities for work. In both the public and private sectors, hiring regulations and practices tend to exclude ex-offenders in subtle and sometimes not so subtle ways. The only available jobs are often undemanding, unattractive, and unrewarding, offering the offender little inducement to turn from criminal behavior.

BARRIERS IN THE PRIVATE SECTOR

In the private sector, few firms exclude ex-offenders as a blanket policy; but their selection criteria tend to have the same effect. For instance, a carefully selected sample of a hundred businesses in Alabama was investigated to determine hiring practices. While only 5 percent of the businesses claimed specifically that they would not hire ex-offenders, a large percentage expressed preferences which would indirectly screen them out (Table 9). It is especially noteworthy

Table 9. Employers' Reasons for Not Hiring Ex-Offenders

Barrier	Percent
Lack of bonding	26.8
No previous experience in hiring ex-offenders	37.2
Lack of good attitude toward work and authority	43.4
Employers require personal interview	44.2
Employers prefer not to hire those committing specific crimes such as armed robbery or narcotics violations	53.0
Long sentences served in prison	54.5
Employers prefer not to hire older ex-offenders	54.6
Lack of basic educational skills	65.1
Will not advance money for tools, licenses	65.5
Prefer not to hire recidivists	74.5
Prefer not to hire ex-offenders who have not been involved in rehabilitation program	76.5

SOURCE: John McKee et al., *Barriers to the Employment of Released Male Offenders* (Elmore, Alabama: Rehabilitation Research Foundation, 1970), p. 22

that one of the most frequent reasons for not hiring offenders is the demand for higher levels of education and participation in rehabilitation programs, suggesting that education and training in prison are vital.

Licensing and bonding requirements affect only a minority of all businesses, but they tend to preclude the hiring of ex-offenders within this minority. Bonds are required in many service and retail jobs; and commercial bonding firms are generally reluctant to cover anyone with a criminal record, specifically excluding them in many policies. Licensing restrictions are perhaps an even greater barrier. The 1960 census found that more than 7 million people were working in occupations that were licensed in some jurisdiction. A survey of licensing statutes in 1970 found that as many as half may be affected by the existence of a criminal record, with many requiring "good moral character," and others specifically excluding persons with felony records.[80]

The most significant barrier to employment in the private sector is, however, the employer's attitude toward offenders. While valid reasons may be given for excluding offenders—for instance, the unavailability of bonds—exclusion will not necessarily end if a bond is provided or other barriers are overcome. Employers are no different than the rest of society, which refuses to recognize that the offender has served his debt and that unless he is given a chance he may be driven back to crime. The intractability of these attitudes can only be measured once the more tangible barriers (and the excuses they provide) are eliminated. If every offender were given education, training, bonding assistance, and licenses, it is likely that he would still have significantly fewer job opportunities than the nonoffender.

It is dangerous, however, to cavalierly dismiss the attitudes of employers as entirely unwarranted—for instance, by applying the same arguments which may be valid in regard to racially discriminatory hiring patterns. With their past failures, innate handicaps, and isolation from the labor market, offenders might on the average make less productive workers than nonoffenders unless they receive special attention, and perhaps even if they do receive special attention. For instance, follow-up studies of releasees reveal frequent job changing;[81] and there is some evidence that those who are given training are even more likely than others to quit their jobs, in part because of too high expectations.[82] The high rates of recidivism also produce unstable work patterns. The FBI survey of persons arrested in 1963 found that 43 percent were rearrested by the end of 1964, and for most this probably meant dismissal from the job.[83] Unless the recidivism can be dramatically reduced, employers in any but the most peripheral jobs will be reluctant to hire and invest time and money in training ex-offenders.

BARRIERS IN THE PUBLIC SECTOR

While it might be expected that the public sector would lead the way in hiring ex-offenders since it bears the responsibility for their rehabilitation and the costs of their failure, barriers to employment are at least as forbidding here as in the private sector. In hiring, most states, counties, and cities ask questions about prior offense records. Perhaps most distressing, 54 percent of the states, 55 percent of the counties, and 77 percent of the large cities require applicants to disclose arrest records even when they were not followed by conviction. Few state that such a record will not automatically disqualify an applicant, and few specifically exclude juvenile offenses and minor crimes. Civil service statutes and regulations use this information to screen out offenders. About a third of all jurisdictions declare that an incorrect answer in application forms is a basis for rejecting an applicant, and this may weed out offenders lying about their record. Two out of five jurisdictions authorize the exclusion of applicants deemed unfit, often for "inferior" or "infamous" conduct.[84]

The real barrier, however, is in the strict practices exercised by most personnel offices. More than 9 out of 10 states, counties, and large cities regularly request a photograph of the applicant, which is referred to the local police or the FBI; more than half take fingerprints and refer them to the police.[85] In terms of hiring, most jurisdictions have "partially restricted policies," making a judgment in each case about the seriousness of offense, its relationship to the intended job, and the indications of rehabilitation. Many police and corrections departments are totally restricted and exclude all persons with criminal records (Table 10).

OPENING JOBS

Those jobs which are foreclosed by specific licensing or bonding requirements might be opened to some degree by changes in licensing regulations and by the provision of bond to offenders. Little effort has been exerted in the first direc-

Table 10. Government and Agency Hiring Policies regarding Persons with Criminal Records

		(in percent)	
	Unrestricted	*Partially Restricted*	*Totally Restricted*
State	31	63	6
County	14	69	16
City	15	76	9
Police	5	28	67
Corrections	28	45	27
Total	15	54	31

SOURCE: Institute of Criminal Law and Procedure, Georgetown University Law Center, "The Effect of a Criminal Record on Employment with State and Local Public Agencies," mimeographed, May 1971, p. 97.

tion, since regulations are usually set locally and often by vested interest groups. There is no way these can be changed except through continuing and conscientious efforts by national trade associations, labor, and the public sector, combined with pressure from the corrections system to link its training programs to the reform of outside labor market practices.

Bonding, on the other hand, can be and is being provided by the federal government. Since March 1966 the Manpower Administration of the U.S. Department of Labor has paid for privately issued bonds on ex-offenders and now offers this nationally through the Employment Service to any who want it and can demonstrate that no other source is available. As of December 31, 1970, 2,645 persons had been bonded in some twenty Concentrated Employment Program cities. The program is now bonding about 60 persons a month and is receiving about 48 terminations, maintaining an average of about 800 bondees on the rolls. Only a small number of claims have been paid; and as a result of the program's favorable experience, the private bond contractor has lowered its rates to very near the competitive level. There is no doubt that this bond helped most of the recipients get jobs which would otherwise have been unavailable, and that it made some contribution to their employment status. The cost now runs about $7 per month per person.[86]

Bonding and license reforms may open up a limited number of jobs, but negative employer attitudes must be overcome if any significant number of ex-offenders are to be helped. Experience with Job Opportunities in the Business Sector and other programs in which the private sector took an active interest demonstrated that some marginal changes could be made by combining exhortation, market pressure, and federal subsidies. There were undoubtedly a number of ex-offenders hired under JOBS, though no records have been kept; and this mechanism might be used on a wider scale. Nevertheless, it is unlikely that employers will participate as actively in a program for ex-offenders as for the "deserving" disadvantaged, especially when they are already serving the latter group.

A much more straightforward solution is to restrict access to criminal records under certain conditions, such as a clean record on the part of the offender for several years. The arguments are especially compelling for eliminating juvenile arrest records after some given amount of time, since for many youths, especially those in disadvantaged neighborhoods, minor crime and arrest are simply a part of growing up. Assurances must be provided that those persons with a genuine need to know about prior arrest can gain access to records, but that those who do not would be excluded.

Public employer practices are not much easier to change than those of private employers, and the reform of civil service laws and personnel procedures is likely to be a slow and arduous process requiring legislative changes, general education, and administrative pressure. The U.S. Civil Service Commission has started to liberalize its rules, and currently the American Bar Association is being funded by the Department of Labor to help state and local jurisdictions identify and eliminate the artificial barriers to employing offenders. The effectiveness of such efforts should not be minimized. To give them some teeth, however, federal grants-in-aid could demand open hiring policies relative to offenders.

CHANGING THE SYSTEM

While artificial barriers to the employment of ex-offenders should be eliminated, structural measures alone are not likely to drastically improve the lot of this group. The massive social legislation of the Great Society attempted to open doors for the disadvantaged; but despite millions of dollars of expenditures and several years of effort, the gains have been limited. Helping an even more disadvantaged clientele will be difficult, especially when the first task is nowhere near completed. What we have learned is that it is not enough to change laws and to urge desirable actions—strong incentives are needed to lead thousands of public and private decision-makers in the desired directions. For instance, employers are unlikely to substantially alter their hiring practices unless offenders are available who are better trained and better educated, and unless there is a subsidy involved to cover any extra training costs and to insure against any extra risk.

Even if employers would change their practices, the problems of offenders would not be immediately overcome. For one thing, many of the restrictions are in the more highly skilled jobs for which few offenders would qualify even with training. For another thing, offenders often get around these barriers on their own, and removing them would have little impact. A survey of federal releasees showed that in two-fifths of the cases employers did not know about the offender's record.[87] The proportion is likely to be much higher for those offenders whose sentences were suspended or dismissed. Obviously, a large number of employers are now hiring offenders without knowing it.

And whatever structural changes are made, it will still remain a fact that offenders are disadvantaged, unlikely to succeed in the world of work unless their handicaps are overcome. Those who go to prison will have the added difficulties which come with stigmatization and removal from the labor market. Structural measures can only work around these more basic problems. However, if these measures can be achieved at a low cost, they are certainly worthwhile.

Employing Offenders in the Public Sector

There is no hard evidence, but it is undoubtedly true, that offenders were hard hit by the rising unemployment in 1970–72. To the degree that they are at the end of the labor queue, they probably found it more difficult than ever to compete with other labor force participants and to find and hold jobs. In 1964, the latest year for which aggregate data are available, the unemployment rate among federal releasees was 16 percent, while the national male civilian unemployment rate was less than 5 percent. Today unemployment is even higher; and due to changes in the structure of the economy, there is probably a decreasing number of jobs for the poorly educated and unskilled. In all likelihood, as many as a fifth of all recently released prisoners are now unemployed; and among all other groups of offenders, employment problems are severe.

Not only are the problems intensified in periods of high unemployment, but the means of dealing with them may be weakened. Evidence from the manpower programs suggests that in slack labor markets training, placement, and job development tend to be less effective than when there are a number of unfilled jobs.[88] Most of the offender manpower projects which have been discussed so far were operating under relatively favorable aggregate conditions, turning out the participants into the tight labor markets of 1968, 1969, and early 1970. It is doubtful that the projects could have had an equal impact on the employability of offenders under current conditions. For instance, in the Manhattan Court Employment Project, which has continued up to the present, placements have dropped from 270 in the first year, to 219 in the second, and 135 in the third, even though efforts have apparently improved as judged by placements per referral. The simple fact is that fewer employers are willing to talk to, much less hire, disadvantaged offenders when more qualified, attractive candidates are available.[89]

Given the difficulties of training, placing, and overcoming job obstacles for offenders in even the best of times, it might well be questioned whether large-scale efforts along these lines are expedient in a slack economy. Crystal ball-gazing is hazardous, but it looks like the economy will remain at a 5 to 5.5 percent rate of aggregate unemployment for some time. This being the case, the real need of offenders may be jobs rather than training or placement.

PUBLIC EMPLOYMENT ALTERNATIVES

The most direct way to provide jobs is to hire offenders for positions in the public sector. Even in the best of times, public employment may be needed if the most seriously disadvantaged are to be put to work. There are, however, a number of conceptually different public employment strategies.

First, transitional jobs could be provided which would serve as a stepping stone to permanent positions in the public sector. This is the idea behind the Emergency Employment Act of 1971 (EEA), which provided one billion dollars to state and local governments to hire the unemployed and disadvantaged for temporary jobs, with the expectation they would move to permanent payrolls. Under this program, guidelines were issued which specifically stated that criminal records should not be an impediment to employment, and it is likely that some offenders will now be hired who would otherwise have been excluded. Greater assistance could be provided if a portion of EEA slots were reserved for offenders or if extra funds were provided for this purpose.

Second, "new careers" could be opened in the public sector for offenders, carefully structured to provide them with the education, training, and experience needed for advancement. One possible source of such jobs is the corrections system itself. In 1966 the Commission on Law Enforcement and the Administration of Justice found that despite the employment of more than 120,000 persons, correctional agencies were grossly understaffed. Personnel for handling parolees and probationers, in particular, were in short supply. The commission estimated that employment would have to more than double by 1975 to meet the current national needs, requiring the recruitment of 30,000 annually. While many of these jobs would require intensive training and experience, the majority, which involve only limited skills, could be filled from the offender population. Paraprofessional positions could also be created which would train offenders to move into more prestigious jobs.[90] A few steps have been taken in this direction. Under New Careers, a program initiated under the Economic Opportunity Act of 1964 to provide paroprofessional career opportunities for the disadvantaged, some ex-offenders have been hired and trained as guards and counselors within prisons. The Manhattan Court and Crossroads Projects used some ex-offender paraprofessionals, claiming that their ability to understand and communicate with the clientele made them effective counselors. If federal funds were provided for correctional manpower, a proportion could be reserved for the hiring of ex-offenders.

Third, temporary jobs could be provided on a continuing basis for offenders immediately after their release from prison or jail. These positions would serve as a short-term holding action until permanent placements could be made in the public or private sector, much the same as the Neighborhood Youth Corps now operates for hard-to-employ youths who are out of school. The emphasis of the temporary jobs for offenders would be on education, training, placement, and income maintenance in combination with work experience to ease the transition back into the labor market.

Fourth, public service jobs could be used as an alternative to jail, at least for misdemeanants. This is a concept which is being considered in Great Britain and makes a great deal of sense if productive jobs can be found which would utilize labor otherwise wasted in prison or jail.

THE POTENTIAL OF PUBLIC EMPLOYMENT

In current economic conditions, the arguments for public employment efforts for offenders are compelling. There is no question that some productive jobs can be created to utilize the talents of otherwise unemployed offenders and to provide them meaningful opportunities for self-improvement. The questions are how many such jobs can be created and how many offenders can be helped.

If the experience with the Emergency Employment Act is any indication, the public sector can absorb a large number of unemployed in transitional jobs—140,000 were put to work within seven months. But it is unlikely that anywhere near this number of offenders could be helped. Many localities would balk at hiring ex-offenders (only a small percentage of the persons hired under EEA apparently have criminal records). This would be especially true if they were expected to move these persons on to permanent payrolls. Under the EEA there has been a great reluctance to change or bend existing hiring policies even for the more "deserving" unemployed. And where ex-offenders have been hired, the results have not been such to generate enthusiasm elsewhere. In Washington, D.C., for instance, where many people hired under EEA had serious criminal records, the majority of early terminations were the result of further involvements with the law.[91]

If federal funds were provided for permanent rather than transitional jobs, localities, states, and federal agencies might be more willing to hire offenders. But the aggregate number of permanent "new careers" should not be exaggerated. For instance, it has been suggested that a large number of ex-offenders could be employed in paraprofessional jobs within the corrections system itself. Besides the fact that there is limited proof of the effectiveness of such workers and the potential market for their services, the reservations of present corrections personnel cannot be totally ignored. There are undoubtedly some risks involved in manning prisons and jails with ex-inmates. And despite the alleged therapeutic benefits of working with others who have similar problems, continued contact with the criminal milieu may be damaging. The number of productive corrections jobs which can be effectively filled by ex-offenders is probably in the hundreds rather than the thousands.

Transitional jobs for recently released prisoners and work programs as alternatives to jail also have limitations. Past experience with public employment of the disadvantaged has failed to demonstrate that useful work can be performed by the relatively unskilled on an intermittent basis. Mostly it results in "make-work" assignments which do little to develop or utilize skills. In the case of work programs for offenders, there is the added danger that they could take on the aura of chain gangs, especially if emphasis is placed on menial labor. And predictably, the public will be aroused when crimes are committed by participant offenders.

These reservations suggest that public employment is not a panacea for the employment difficulties of offenders and that serious problems will be encountered. But these reservations do not dispute the need for expanded efforts. More offenders could be hired under the EEA or a similar program and moved on to well-paying and stable jobs in public service. New careers could be opened in the corrections system for a small but visible number of offenders. Work programs could be initiated which might be an attractive alternative to jail or to public income maintenance during postrelease adjustment. Though there is no concrete proof, it is doubtful that under current economic conditions other manpower services can be as effective as public employment. If anything is to be accomplished, the government will have to take the lead by providing jobs for those who cannot find work.

Can We Help the Hardest Core?

This brief review and assessment of efforts to increase the employability of offenders leaves little room for more than the most restrained optimism. There have been a wide range of projects to test the effectiveness of various strategies; and though the evidence which has been gathered is limited, very little of it is positive. There is no proof that any single manpower service or strategy has had more than a marginal impact on its recipients, and no proof that any combination of services can make a substantial contribution. Some glimmerings of success have shown through and these should obviously be exploited; but overall, the results have been disappointing. On the basis of the existing evidence, it does not seem likely that the employment problems of offenders can be significantly alleviated by manpower programs, or that these programs will have a noticeable impact on the rate of crime.

This is contrary to what we want to believe. Offenders as a group have severe employment problems. They typically lack training, adequate education, knowledge of job opportunities, work experience, and other essentials to success in the world of work. It is therefore logical to assume that if they were provided specific skills, remedial education, placement assistance, and other manpower services they would show more success. We want to believe that every individual can be helped and that every societal impediment to his improvement can be overcome.

There is also a demonstrated relationship between employment problems and criminal behavior. Those who fail in the world of work are more likely than others to turn to crime, and if they do, to be caught up by the corrections system. It is therefore logical to assume that if offenders could be placed in more stable, attractive, and rewarding jobs, the propensity to commit new crimes would be reduced. We want to believe that something can be done to alleviate the crime problem and to rehabilitate the average offender.

Yet there is meager evidence to sustain these beliefs. The dollars spent to date on manpower services for offenders have had little impact on institutions or individuals. Worse still, they have revealed how intractable the problems are, casting doubt as to whether, even with redirection and expansion, manpower services will have more than a very marginal impact. It is a moot point whether increased employability will lead to reduced recidivism or whether we should be concerned only with helping the individual because he is disadvantaged regardless of the effect on criminal behavior. The depressing fact is that we have not yet demonstrated our capacity to increase employability among offenders to any significant degree.

This does not prove that the employment problems of prisoners and releasees as well as probationers, offenders awaiting trial, and reformed ex-offenders cannot or should not be ameliorated. The evidence so far is inconclusive. Every insight which has been gained is qualified by an "if" or "but," and every statement can be questioned. The evidence can also be interpreted in different ways depending on one's preconceptions. No interpretation is completely right or wrong, and vastly different policy prescriptions might be derived from different readings of the same facts.

Thus, there are three courses of action which might be taken at the present juncture: manpower programs for offenders could be dramatically expanded on an operational level, curtailed or at least maintained at the present level, or modestly expanded on an experimental basis until there is greater evidence of success. There are sound arguments for all three courses.

On the one hand, experience has shown that the corrections system, the offender population, and society as a whole will not readily change their actions and attitudes. There are so many interrelated problems in dealing with offenders and so many obstacles to overcome that massively increased resources may be needed to accomplish dramatic change. The disappointing impact of previous programs may have resulted from their limited scale. It is also true that these programs were testing out new ideas and that full-scale undertakings which build on the programs' strengths and avoid their shortcomings will be more effective. From this perspective, previous experimental efforts have demonstrated the basic feasibility of serving offenders and the alternative approaches which may be pursued more effectively and have provided the foundation for improved performance.

At the opposite extreme, experience has failed to show that an investment in offenders will yield a very high rate of return—for instance, as compared with manpower services for less disadvantaged groups. Those who feel that offenders do not deserve special attention—or rather, that they warrant inattention—will be understandably reluctant to allocate further resources to previously unsuccessful or, at most, modestly successful efforts. If intensive commitments of time, money, and manpower have not significantly alleviated the employment problems of offenders or altered their behavior patterns, it may be naive to pin any hope on more effective implementation on an expanded basis.

Depending on one's predilections, it is easy to follow either extreme. However, the middle ground might be the most effective for public policy. On the one hand, policymakers should resist the temptation to expand dramatically into areas where the evidence indicates scarce resources will have a limited impact. Whatever the political expediency of initiating massive programs for offenders and no matter how sincere the belief that offenders must be helped, money should not be spent if it will do no good. On the other hand, policymakers should also resist the temptation to turn their backs on the problem completely. If the effort to test out new ideas ended with every failure, we would not get very far. We do not now know enough to say that manpower services cannot significantly benefit offenders.

The middle road between these extremes is to continue experimentation on a larger scale while proceeding to the operational implementation of those strategies which demonstrate the greatest promise. To this end, new approaches would be tested; the less effective would be modified; and those with potential for success would be expanded. There would be no "across-the-board" expansion of manpower efforts, but rather a selective implementation based on monitoring and evaluation of performance.

TAKING STOCK

If this middle road is followed, the first step is to take stock of what we now know about the effectiveness of the various strategies and approaches which have been tested. Any judgments at this time are necessarily tentative and impressionistic, but until more can be learned, they must serve as a guide for public policy. The following, then, are the general lessons which seem to be suggested by the admittedly limited experience with manpower programs for offenders.

1) Pretrial intervention can be an effective way of reaching first and second offenders who are not yet committed to a life of crime. Manpower services apparently work best with those in their early twenties who have not been able to get a foothold in the world of work but who have matured out of their teenage life style. Careful screening of the clientele is necessary, for instance, to weed out drug users, who need other help in addition to manpower services, and those with other severe employment problems who need sustained and intensive assistance. It is imperative also that pretrial projects be worked out with the court and corrections systems to insure close cooperation. With these caveats, it appears likely that the modest success of experimental pretrial programs can be replicated.

2) Intensive vocational training in prison can be made to work. However, the lackluster record of prison training in the past suggests that there are formidable obstacles which must

be overcome. Because of scarce resources, the physical isolation of prisoners, the deficiencies of inmates selected for training, the lack of supportive services, and the antagonism of prison staffs, vocational training has to be carefully implemented. Prisoners must be selected on the basis of their ability to benefit from training rather than their seniority, docility, or expendability from prison work. Supportive services are needed, especially job development and placement, to insure that trainees apply what they have learned. And, perhaps most vitally, the prison staff must be involved in and committed to the training program.

3) Basic educational efforts in prisons utilizing new methods and technologies can apparently increase the educational achievement of disadvantaged offenders. Many of the bright but undermotivated can be helped with GED coursework, and the diploma itself is a valuable credential in the labor market. A small but important minority can also benefit from college extension work and eventually "college release." Prisons might be more effective emphasizing education for employment rather than vocational training and other job-related services.

4) The prison labor force is grossly underutilized, which is a loss to society and to the individuals. Work experience and on-the-job training can be provided in prison jobs both in industries and in maintenance of the institution. A minority of prison industries, most often in federal prisons, are highly efficient and provide the worker with valuable skills. There is no reason why these cannot be replicated elsewhere, but the impetus must come largely from the separate state corrections systems. Federal funds might be used to attract some businesses on or near prisons, as in other depressed areas; however, the effectiveness of this approach remains to be proved. Currently at the federal level, an Executive Order restricts the purchase of products made in state prisons; and

various state laws restrict the sale and transport of prison-made goods. If prison industries are to be expanded, these restrictions have to be reviewed and modified, though they must still give adequate protection to "outside" labor to prevent unfair competition.

5) Work release should be more widely utilized. When an offender can earn money for himself and pay back the costs of maintenance while remaining under the supervision of the prison, everyone benefits. Though some prisoners may escape or commit crimes while on work release, the number to date has been manageable—less than the number of parolees recidivating or violating the terms of their parole. The major impediment to expansion is administrative rather than legislative, and all correctional personnel (especially those in local jails) should be urged to experiment with this approach on a selective basis. Manpower services are needed on an expanded scale by work releasees. Efforts should be made to find meaningful jobs, to provide transportation, and to help the worker and the employer with any problems.

6) Efforts to provide intensive manpower services during postrelease adjustment have not been very successful. Adult offenders need a job; and having just gotten out of prison, they are not receptive to further counseling and discipline. Residential institutions may be valuable when resources are limited, but a preferable strategy might be to provide more adequate income maintenance during the transition period. Teenage ex-prisoners and those in their early twenties have much more serious adjustment problems, which definitely must be addressed if the related massive rates of recidivism are to be reduced; but efforts to increase employability are apparently not the key.

7) Placement and job development services can improve the work experience of ex-prisoners, especially when these services are more intensive than the normal Employment

Service efforts and are linked to rehabilitation and training programs within the prison. Careful observation of the on-going Employment Service experiments providing aid to offenders should indicate whether this is an effective delivery agency for such assistance.

8) The conceptual arguments for income maintenance during postrelease adjustment are compelling; but as yet, there is little evidence of its impact on recidivism. Ongoing experiments will have to be closely watched to determine whether money alone, or in conjunction with services, is worthwhile. Experience has already demonstrated, however, that lump-sum or periodic payments will be squandered unless they are structured as incentives for desired types of action.

9) Many of the employment problems of ex-offenders are intensified by artificial barriers in the public and private sector. Ex-offenders are often denied private bonding (which is a requisite for many jobs) even though experience with federal bonding programs has demonstrated that the risk is not much higher than for nonoffenders. Licensing requirements and civil service regulations exclude ex-offenders, even where their criminal record has no relevance to their job performance. Private employers tend to discriminate against offenders in practice if not in principle, too. These impediments are difficult to eliminate. Though bonding has been successfully expanded, hiring practices cannot be easily changed since they involve thousands upon thousands of separate decisionmakers who are difficult to regulate. The combined strategies of exhortation, market pressure, subsidies, and revised laws and regulations used to ameliorate the barriers facing other disadvantaged groups can be used here. These strategies are a vital ingredient for helping offenders.

10) With their personal deficiencies and the added handicap of their criminal records, offenders are usually at the end

of the labor queue—the last to be hired and the first to be fired. In slack labor markets, their employment problems become even more severe, while training, placement and job development efforts to help with these problems become less effective. The obvious solution is to provide jobs in the public sector. There are several different public employment strategies ranging from "make work" jobs during the post-release transition to new careers in corrections and other areas of public service. Despite the meager experience with such efforts, and despite the problems which can be anticipated, public employment programs for offenders are warranted, if for no other reason than the shortcomings of other approaches.

THE BROADER IMPLICATIONS

While experimental manpower efforts have yielded new insights into the effectiveness of particular services and strategies, the broader implications are perhaps even more significant in determining manpower policies for offenders.

The most basic lesson is that, to be effective, manpower programs must be implemented aggressively and innovatively. To begin with, offenders are an extremely disadvantaged clientele who are often alienated, unreceptive, and difficult to help in even the best of circumstances. Their personal problems are complicated by contact with the corrections system. Understaffed and underfunded, court personnel, parole and probation officers, and prison staffs can barely fulfill their assigned missions. They are usually opposed to any new efforts that add to their duties without adding to their resources; and some may be opposed to rehabilitation measures which they equate with "coddling prisoners." This antipathy toward offenders exists at all levels in society. Whether it is justified or not, many employers and policymakers as well as police, court, and corrections personnel (and even manpower experts) doubt whether offenders can be rehabilitated or whether they deserve the attention which rehabilitation requires. This negative attitude can be a greater impediment to the success of manpower services than any identifiable problem in the system or the individual.

Often public policy follows the path of least resistance. Given the formidable obstacles which exist, this course would be fatal in designing manpower programs and policies for offenders. For instance, when money was handed out to the prisons to initiate special vocational training programs, the prisons tended to carry out business as usual, and the programs had little impact; when the money was used as part of an innovative effort for institutional change involving both outsiders and the prison staff, it was much more successful. Likewise, it is probably not enough to give probation and parole offices money to hire job developers and counselors or to give the Employment Service added personnel to serve offenders. Changes in methods and approaches must be achieved.

Institutional change does not occur without attractive incentives. The court and corrections systems cannot be expected to take on new functions or to do things in new ways unless money is provided, and strings are attached. Marginal subsidies and temporary projects are likely to have little impact.

To provide these incentives, more resources are needed. The public must be convinced that such efforts are worthwhile and may prove highly effective. Though there has been some shift in public attitude away from the punishment and detention philosophy of corrections toward the recognition of the need for rehabilitation, disaffection will come quickly if rehabilitation is not achieved. Manpower programs must justify themselves primarily on the grounds of improving employability; but if they have no impact on recidivism, continued public support is unlikely.

Given the demand for immediate results, the danger is to expand programs on the basis of inflated promises and roseate assessments. The ax will fall quickly if this approach is taken in serving offenders. What is needed, instead, is an admission that we still do not have the answers and that only modest achievements can be expected in dealing with such a disadvantaged clientele. The urgency of the offender problem should provide the impetus for action rather than bold claims about our ability to solve it. The unfortunate reality is that there are not as yet any proven solutions. The main thing we have learned from the experimental manpower efforts is that there is a lot which is not yet known about dealing with offenders. Their employment problems may be similar to those of other disadvantaged groups, but offenders must be ministered to in different ways. Consideration must be given not only to manpower issues but also those of crime and corrections. Experience is limited, and both corrections and manpower personnel have much to learn from each other.

THE MIDDLE ROAD

Public action cannot be delayed, however, until everything we would like to know has been learned. Neither should it proceed by ignoring the lessons of the past, especially when they are negative. The most effective public policy is likely to be one which combines experimentation and measured expansion. If this middle road is taken, the following lines of action would be pursued.

First, *greater effort would be exerted towards monitoring and evaluating existing programs.* For instance, nothing is known about the number and success of ex-offenders in existing manpower programs. Despite several investigations, there is little comprehensive knowledge about the effectiveness of prison institutions or training. And too few projects follow-up their participants in any longitudinal way to discover if the services have a long-run impact.

Second, *new strategies would be put to the test, and the gaps in our knowledge filled.* As examples, we have not yet done much for probationers, and projects should be initiated offering them manpower services. Competitive industries might be attracted in or near a few prisons to test the effectiveness of such projects. Training release might be offered to prisoners for participation in community manpower programs. Manpower specialists might be assigned to the court to aid in the disposition of cases.

Third, *improvements would be made in the existing experimental methods.* The method used by the Department of Labor in testing the MDTA approach is optimal: from a limited number of projects demonstrating the feasibility of a strategy, it proceeded to implementation on a broader scale with a standardized approach and reporting procedure which facilitated comparison and measurement. Too many agencies are now funding too many projects. The results are scattered, poorly evaluated, and difficult to assess in any aggregate way. Some jurisdictional lines should be established so that the various agencies funding projects can avoid duplication as much as possible; mechanisms for coordination and communication will have to be established.

Fourth, *greater emphasis would be placed on institutional change.* Some of the experimental and demonstration projects have led to reform of the corrections system. For instance, the Draper Project in Alabama had a very marked impact on the integration of Alabama prison facilities. With proper oversight and control, and more careful planning for this purpose, greater leverage could be exerted with the federal dollar to permanently change the existing system.

Too often now, services are provided as long as the federal spigots are turned on, and then the projects dry up.

Fifth, *some services should be expanded.* There is no guarantee that any particular approach will work on a large scale, but several strategies warrant more widespread implementation. Pretrial intervention has been successful to some degree in curbing recidivism and increasing employability. The experimental projects should be replicated in other areas. Work release has also been relatively successful, and manpower services are needed to provide counseling, placement, and follow-up for participants, as well as an incentive for the prisons to implement such an approach. Programmed learning and higher education in prisons have also indicated some degree of effectiveness and can be expanded. Public employment programs for offenders can be initiated on at least a limited scale with a fair assurance of success. And as other approaches demonstrate some success on the experimental and demonstration level, they should be expanded as rapidly as possible to find out whether they can work on a broader scale.

Sixth, *greater selectivity must be exercised in choosing participants for offender manpower programs.* Even if there are no entirely accurate predictors of success, enough has been learned to do a better job of choosing participants. Hard-core drug addicts are apparently not a good bet, though nonaddicted drug users might benefit significantly; teenagers do not seem to gain from manpower services, though they can clearly benefit from other approaches; and the chances of success vary inversely with the number of previous arrests so that recurrent offenders should probably be excluded. However, rules of selection must be applied with flexibility based on case-by-case assessments of motivation and innate potential.

Finally, *earlier intervention strategies should probably be stressed.* All indications are that manpower services are more effective the earlier they enter into the life of the offender. Primary emphasis should, therefore, be given to pretrial and probation programs as well as to other efforts for first and second offenders. Experimentation must continue at all levels; and if success is demonstrated, efforts should certainly be expanded. We should not give up on those who are the most deeply involved in crime and corrections, but we should not allocate massive resources without proof that they will have a positive impact.

Even such modest actions would require substantially increased resources. Experimentation on a scale which will yield some fairly unequivocal answers—for instance, on the order of the 251 MDTA investment—is costly; but this is the only way to really find out whether the success of isolated E&D projects can be replicated. On the other hand, experimentation implies trying out an idea on less than a full-scale, operational basis. A doubling of the Labor Department's present $30 million investment could accomplish most of the modest goals which have been outlined, while the $100 to $200 million of the Javits-Esch bill, divided among the numerous strategies it authorizes, might still be considered an experimental effort—at least in the sense that it would reach only a small portion of the universe of need.

Whatever judgment is made, it should not be based on any inflated hope of success in increasing employability or reducing recidivism among offenders. A substantial investment may be justified to find out what will and will not work, but it is not justified on the basis of the performance record of previous investments.

The fact remains that human as well as natural resources have little value if they cannot be recovered and put to use.

The waste and the potential of the offender are obvious, and continued efforts are needed to reduce the former and realize the latter. But if manpower services do no good, they themselves are a waste of resources which could be better applied somewhere else.

Notes

OFFENDERS AND THE CORRECTIONS SYSTEM

1. Federal Bureau of Investigation, *Uniform Crime Reports for the United States, 1969* (Washington, D.C.: U.S. Government Printing Office, 1970), pp. 98–99.

2. George A. Pownall, "Employment Problems of Released Prisoners," mineographed (University of Maryland, College Park, Md., 1969), p. 137.

3. FBI, *Crime Reports, 1969*, pp. 122–23.

4. Pownall, "Employment Problems."

5. U.S. Department of Commerce, Bureau of the Census, *Statistical Abstract of the United States, 1971* (Washington, D.C.: U.S. Government Printing Office, 1971), pp. 155–59.

6. The President's Commission on Law Enforcement and Administration of Justice, *Task Force Report: Corrections* (Washington, D.C.: U.S. Government Printing Office, 1967).

7. Abt Associates, Inc., *An Evaluation of MDTA Training in Correctional Institutions,* vols. 1, 2, 3, and Final Summary (Washington, D.C.: AAI, May 1971), pp. 35– 36.

8. Pownall, "Employment Problems," p. 107.

9. Center for the Study of Crime, Delinquency, and Corrections, *Study of Adequacy of Prisoner Work-Release Law and Related Regulations,* Proposal to the Department of Labor, mimeographed, p. 4.

10. Bureau of the Census, *Statistical Abstract, 1971* p. 158.

111

EMPLOYMENT PROBLEMS OF OFFENDERS

11. Daniel Glaser and Ken Rice, "Crime, Age, and Unemployment," *American Sociological Review* 24 (October 1959): 679–86.

12. Belton M. Fleisher, "The Effect of Unemployment on Delinquent Behavior," *Journal of Political Economics* 61 (1963): 543–55.

13. E. H. Sutherland and Donald R. Cressy, *Principles of Criminology* (New York: J. B. Lippincott Company, 1966), pp. 235–38.

14. Nathan Glaser, *The Effectiveness of a Prison and Parole System* (New York: The Bobbs-Merrill Company, Inc., 1964), pp. 232–59; and Robert Evans, "The Labor Market and Parole Success," *Journal of Human Resources* 3, no. 2 (Spring 1968).

15. Abt Associates, *Evaluation of MDTA Training*, vol. 3.

16. Pownall, "Employment Problems."

17. Bureau of Labor Statistics, *Educational Attainment of Workers, March 1969, 1970*, Special Labor Force Report 125 (Washington, D.C.: U.S. Government Printing Office, 1970).

SERVICES FOR OFFENDERS

18. John J. Galvin, "Training Correctional Manpower," *Manpower* (January 1971), p. 15.

19. John P. Conrad, "A Compilation of Ongoing and Contemplated Research in Corrections and Rehabilitation," mimeographed (Interagency Council on Corrections, August 1971), p. 2.

20. U.S. Senate Subcommittee on Employment, Manpower, and Poverty, *Reform of Federally Funded Manpower Training Programs*, 92d Cong., 1st sess., December 1971, p. 147.

ALTERNATIVES TO INCARCERATION

21. Commission on Law Enforcement and Administration of Justice, *Corrections*, p. 27.

22. *Ibid.*, p. 30.

23. Vera Institute of Justice, *The Manhattan Court Employment Project* (New York: Vera Institute of Justice, 1970).

24. Vera Institute of Justice, "Final Report of the Manhattan Court Employment Project," mimeographed, December 1971, pp. 25–26.

25. Vera Institute of Justice, "Quarterly Report, March 1, 1971, to June 30, 1971," mimeographed, p. 6.

26. Roberta Rovner-Pieczenik, *Project Crossroads as Pre-Trial Intervention: A Program Evaluation* (Washington, D.C.: National Committee for Children and Youth, 1970).

27. John F. Holahan, *A Benefit-Cost Analysis of Project Crossroads* (Washington, D.C.: National Committee for Children and Youth, December 1970), p. 63.

28. Glen C. Cain. "Benefit-Cost Estimate of Job Corps," mimeographed, (Office of Economic Opportunity, May 22, 1967).

29. Rovner-Pieczenik, *Project Crossroads.*

30. Subcommittee on Employment, Manpower, and Poverty, *Reform of Training Programs*, p. 135.

31. Bertram Johnson, "The 'Failure' of a Parole Research Project," *California Youth Authority Quarterly* 18 (1965): 35–39.

32. Palmer, Neto et al., *Community Treatment Project, Seventh Progress Report* (San Francisco: California Youth Authority, 1968).

33. James Robinson and Gerlad Smith, "The Effectiveness of Correctional Programs," *Crime and Delinquency* (January 1970).

VOCATIONAL TRAINING IN PRISONS

34. *The Total Impact of Manpower Programs: A Four-City Case Study* (Washington, D.C.: Olympus Research Corporation, 1971).

35. Clyde E. Sullivan and Wallace Mandell, *Restoration of Youth through Training* (New York: Wakoff Research Center, 1967), pp. 11–12.

36. Address by Secretary of Labor James Hodgson to the American Bar Association, Commission on Correctional Facilities and Services April 13, 1971, News Release 71-209, U.S. Department of Labor, p. 6.

37. Abt Associates, *Evaluation of MDTA Training.*

38. Sullivan and Mandell, *Restoration of Youth*, pp. 12–13.

39. *Ibid.*, p. 136–41.

40. *Ibid.*, p. 331.

41. *Ibid.*, p. 150.

42. Abt Associates, *Evaluation of MDTA Training*, vol. 3, pp. 29–34.

43. *Manpower Report of the President, 1970* (Washington, D.C.: U.S. Government Printing Office, 1970), p. 308.

44. Abt Associates, *Evaluation of MDTA Training*, vol. 2.

45. David Lewen, "Memorandum for Record Concerning the Evaluation of MDTA-Funded Experimental Training, Programs in Correctional Institutions Performed by Abt Associates," mimeographed, (Columbia University, October 1971).

46. Abt Associates, *Evaluation of MDTA Training*, vol. 3.

EDUCATION FOR EMPLOYMENT

47. George Pownall, "Employment Problems of Released Prisoners," *Manpower*, January 1971, pp. 30–31.

48. Abt Associates, *Evaluation of MDTA Training*, vol. 3, p. 30.

49. John McKee, *The Draper Project, MDTA Experimental and Demonstration Findings No. 6* (Washington, D.C.: U.S. Government Printing Office, 1971), p. 24.

50. John McKee et al., *Barriers to the Employment of Released Male Offenders* (Elmore, Alabama: Rehabilitation Research Foundation, 1970), p. 22.

51. Abt Associates, *Evaluation of MDTA Training*, vol. 2, p. 36.

52. Sar A. Levitan, *The Great Society's Poor Law* (Baltimore: The Johns Hopkins Press, 1970), p. 294.

53. McKee, *The Draper Project*, pp. 74–79.

54. *Ibid.*, p. 14.

55. Birch Bayh, "Omnibus Correctional Reform Act of 1971," *Congressional Record* (November 22, 1971), pp. X19365–72.

56. John McKee, *The Draper Project*, p. 113.

WORK IN PRISON

57. "Another Year of Success Reported in Training, Hiring of Prison Inmates," *Federal Times*, February 10, 1971.

58. Abt Associates, *Evaluation of MDTA Training*, vol. 2. p. 33.

59. Sterling Institute, *To Help Men Change* (Washington, D.C.: U.S. Bureau of Prisons, 1970), p. 9.

WORK RELEASE

60. Abt Associates, *Evaluation of MDTA Training*, vol. 2, pp. 38–39.

61. J. Kitchener and W. Lebowitz, "Preliminary Highlights from Work Release Follow-Up Study," mimeographed, (Bureau of Prisons, March 1970).

62. "Information Sheet: Work Release, Study Releases, Home Furlough and LEAA Budgets," mimeographed, (Law Enforcement Assistance Administration, 1971).

63. Kitchener and Lebowitz, "Work Release Follow-Up Study."

64. Allan Berman, "Predicting Success on Work-Release," mimeographed, p. 8.

INTENSIVE POSTRELEASE SERVICES

65. Commission on Law Enforcement and Administration of Justice, *Corrections*, pp. 184–90.

66. International Halfway House Association, *1969 Directory* (Cincinnati, Ohio: The Association, 1969).

67. William Raspberry, "Statistics on Convicts," *Washington Post*, December 20, 1971, p. 19.

68. Leonard Witt, *Project Develop* (New York: New York State Division of Parole, 1969).

INCOME MAINTENANCE DURING POSTRELEASE ADJUSTMENT

69. Daniel Glaser, Eugene S. Zemers, and Charles W. Dean, *Money against Crime: A Survey of Economic Assistance to Released Prisoners* (Chicago: The John Howard Association, 1961).

70. Commission on Law Enforcement and Administration of Justice, *Corrections*, p. 68.

71. Sullivan and Mandell, *Restoration of Youth*, pp. 80–81.

72. McKee, *The Draper Project*, pp. 87–88.

73. E. M. Oliver et al., *A Future for Correctional Rehabilitation?* (Olympia, Wash.: Division of Vocational Rehabilitation, Coordinating Service for Occupational Education, 1969), p. 60.

74. Kenneth Lenihan, "A Proposal to Study the Effects on Ex-Prisoners of Financial Aid and Employment Assistance Programs Designed to Facilitate Post-Release Adjustment," mimeographed, Proposal to Office of Research and Development, Manpower Administration, by Bureau of Social Science Research, 1971.

JOB DEVELOPMENT AND PLACEMENT SERVICES

75. Pownall, "Employment Problems of Released Prisoners," mimeographed (University of Maryland, College Park, Md., 1969).

76. Abt Associates, *Evaluation of MDTA Training*, vol. 2, p. 84.

77. Joseph Gwozdecki, W. Jenkins, and Lynda Hart, *The Incidence of Training-Related Job Placement of Draper Vocational Trainees* (Elmore, Alabama: Rehabilitation Research Foundation, 1970).

78. Gerald Gundersen, *Evaluation Study of the Model Ex-Offender Program*, mimeographed, DSE Report No. 15, June 1971, pp. 35–39.

THE SYSTEMS APPROACH

79. E. M. Oliver et al., *Correctional Rehabilitation*, pp. 83–85.

REMOVING BARRIERS TO EMPLOYMENT

80. Institute of Criminal Law and Procedure, Georgetown University Law Center, "The Effect of a Criminal Record on Employment with State and Local Public Agencies," mimeographed, May 1971, p. 57.

81. Pownall, "Employment Problems," p. 207.

82. Sullivan and Mandell, *Restoration of Youth*, p. 309.

83. FBI, *Crime Reports, 1969,* p. 39.

84. Institute of Criminal Law and Procedure, *Effect of a Criminal Record on Employment* pp. 13–53.

85. *Ibid.*, pp. 97–98.

86. "The Federal Bonding Program," Department of Labor, Manpower Administration, mimeographed, March 1971.

87. Pownall, "Employment Problems," p. 210.

EMPLOYING OFFENDERS IN THE PUBLIC SECTOR

88. Sar A. Levitan and Robert Taggart, *Social Experimentation and Manpower Policy: The Rhetoric and the Reality* (Baltimore: The Johns Hopkins Press, 1971), pp. 72–82.

89. Vera Institute, "Final Report of the Manhattan Court Employment Project, mimeographed, December 1971, p. 91.

90. Galvin, "Training Correctional Manpower," p. 15.

91. Robert Taggart, "The Emergency Employment Act in the District of Columbia," mimeographed, (National Manpower Policy Task Force, December 20, 1971).

Library of Congress Cataloging in Publication Data

Taggart, Robert,1945–
    The prison of unemployment.

    (Policy studies in employment and welfare, no. 14)
    Includes bibliographical references.
    1. Ex-convicts, Employment of. 2. Rehabilitation of criminals. 3. Vocational rehabilitation. I. Title.

HV9288.T33   331.5'1   72–3228
ISBN 0–8018–1424–3
ISBN 0–8018–1425–1 (pbk.)